THE GREAT
SNOW JOB

THE STORY OF
TAXES AND MONEY/
FRAUD AND SLAVERY

BARRIE KONICOV

PUBLISHED BY E.L.I. PRESS
1995

E.L.I. Press
c/o 9392 Whitneyville Rd. SE
Alto, Mich. PZ 49302
(616) 891-2217

ISBN 0-9647197-0-3

Printed and bound in America

DEDICATION

This book is dedicated to each of you who will read it and stand up to the fraud and slavery in our tax and money system.

NOTICE

This book has been written for the express purpose of presenting the author's findings and opinions based on research and analysis of the subject matters covered. The information contained herein is not provided for the purpose of rendering legal or professional opinions or services.

As there is always an element of risk in standing up for one's rights, the author and publisher disclaim any responsibility or liability for any loss which may be incurred as a result of the use and/or application, directly or indirectly, of any of the information contained herein.

TABLE OF CONTENTS

PART II

FOREWORD

The problem is the money. Taxes are a symptom.

There is a movement beginning to catch on in America to replace the current taxing structure with a flat tax. On the surface, this would seem to be a good thing. Those promoting a flat tax point to its obvious advantages over our current system.

Our current taxing system requires over 5.4 billion hours of labor per year just to fill out the I.R.S.'s forms. Currently, it is estimated that the Treasury loses over $200 billion a year in revenue due to the underground economy. A flat tax promises to collect this lost tax revenue. The argument for the flat tax is that everyone would pay his or her fair share. Supporters of the flat tax say that removing the export tax from our products would make them more competitive on the world market. These are just some of the reasons which are given in support of the flat tax.

Those who are pushing for change do not want a majority of the people to know that there is a huge problem in the current system. The problem is that We the People are learning anew the truths of our Constitutional heritage. We are learning that the founders of this country bequeathed to us a system which was free from direct taxation and that, under our current tax system, a tax on our person or our property is a "direct tax." What many of our politicians are hiding is that our current tax and money system is out of harmony with the meaning and intent of the Constitution.

What is now being covered up is that We the People are instituting change. Today there are millions of us dedicated to re-establishing our Constitution as the supreme law of the land. With our Constitution re-established, We the People will be freed from a tax and money system that has made slaves of us all.

Those in power want to stay in power. They know that We the People are catching on to their scheme. Already, the I.R.S. admits that over 20 million of us have stopped filing tax returns. An equally impressive number of us have educated ourselves concerning the fraudulent nature of our tax and money system. To avoid being caught in their web of treason, our politicians are promoting the flat tax as a way of solving our problems.

It has been said that the art of government is creating a problem, misdiagnosing it, and then applying the wrong solution. In no case is that more evident than in the movement for a flat tax. After you have read this book, you will know that the problem is the fraudulent nature of our money system and that the taxes levied upon We the People are a symptom. The solution to the problem is to return this country to its constitutional heritage.

Unless We the People take it upon ourselves to change the system immediately, these are some of the events which I see taking place in the United States.

The stock market will experience a repeat of 1929. Widespread disruption in the financial markets will trigger massive layoffs, collapsing the economy. People will not be able to make their house payments, and banks will rush in to foreclose on the nation. Disruption in the world economy will mean food shortages. This, in turn, will lead to armed conflict in our streets.

These predictions are not new. They are not even mine. Who among us is not aware of the Biblical prophecies? I believe that the purpose of prophecy is to provide a warning and to encourage people to change. The changes I suggest throughout this book are as simple as 1-2-3.

1. Educate yourself on the subject of taxes and money.

2. Take appropriate action, based upon what you have learned.

3. Teach what you have learned to those closest to you.

There is a window of opportunity. And, if We the People change ourselves first, then we can change the system. But, in order to change the system, we must first change ourselves.

THE GREAT
SNOW JOB

PART I

THE STORY
OF TAXES

THE STORY OF TAXES

Imagine with me that you are sitting home one evening and there is a knock at your front door. Opening the door, you find a Mexican soldier with a document in his hand. Although you are somewhat startled, you, nevertheless, invite him into your home. Luckily, you know some Spanish because his English is not very good. But, with his limited English and your limited Spanish, he gets you to understand that he is there to give you your individual INCOME tax return. The form is to be filled out and returned to the Mexican Government with a check for 30% of your last year's earnings by April 15th. What would you do? Most probably, you would be polite but firm, pointing out to the soldier that this is the United States of America, not Mexico, and that he doesn't have any authority to be in this country collecting INCOME taxes.

The soldier is also polite but firm. It doesn't matter to the soldier where you live or who you work for because his job is to collect the tax. After a few uncomfortable moments, you ask the soldier to leave, and he does. After sharing the story with your friends, the incident is forgotten.

Then you receive a notice from the Mexican Government informing you that, because you have not filled out an INCOME tax return, one has been filled out and filed for you. Now, besides the tax, you owe an additional 25% for penalties and interest.

Thinking that this is all a big mistake, you call the number on the form. The people you talk to can barely speak English. Finally, you give up trying to get them to understand you, and you dismiss the entire incident as a big mistake.

A few weeks later, you receive a threatening letter in the mail. The letter is a notice telling you that, unless you pay your tax immediately, legal proceedings will be instigated. You are notified that they have several means of getting you to cooperate. They could place a lien on your home and sell it for back taxes, your wages could be garnished, or you could be facing possible criminal charges if you don't pay the tax. By now, your fear is beginning to rise. You call your attorney and tax accountant and make an appointment to see them.

After looking over the papers, they both agree. The papers are in order. Granted, heretofore the Mexican Government did not have any authority to tax United States citizens directly, but, because of the new North American Free Trade Agreement, they now SAY that they have the authority. Both your attorney and your accountant have been specially trained by the Mexican Government to advise you in matters of this sort. They are confident that everything is legal. They advise you to either pay the tax or run the risk of losing everything and going to jail.

Now you are really angry. After talking it over with your family, you decide to fight the tax. After all, this is America, and you do have rights. On the other hand, how can you beat the Mexican Government? They are *the government*, and the law is on their side. Even if you do win, it will cost more to fight the tax than it would to pay it.

It doesn't matter. You are a person of principle and integrity. Regardless of the cost, you are going to fight this tax. It is obvious to you that the Mexican Government has no right to tax a United States citizen.

The day of the trial you show up in court fearful but confident that everything will turn out in your favor. The Constitution will protect you. Yet, the moment the trial begins, fear takes over. The Mexican Government presents several expert witnesses, each testifying to the truth and accuracy of the documents. As far as they are concerned, you owe the tax.

Your attorney is polite, but he doesn't seem to have much fight in him. He keeps pandering to the judge. Finally, it is your turn to take the witness stand. Then fear really takes over. In the end, the judge rules that the Mexican Government's papers are in order and that you owe what they say you owe. Only, now, the amount has doubled due to penalties and interest. Unable to pay, your home is sold in order to pay the tax, and you are out on the street. To top it off, your attorney keeps telling you how lucky you are, claiming that you could be in jail right now for "willfully failing to file," which is a criminal offense. That is what they do to "tax protesters."

If you are thinking, "Thank God that this is only happening in my imagination," or if you think that this couldn't happen to you because this is America and your rights are protected by the Constitution and the Bill of Rights, you're wrong. It does happen, and it happens every day to people just like you and me. Just as the Mexican Government has no authority to impose an individual INCOME tax on you, neither does the United States Government.

I know that this is true because I have not paid individual INCOME taxes for the past four years. In fact, my wife has a letter from the Internal Revenue Service notifying her that she is not required to file a tax return for a specific tax period. And, during that period, her employment compensation exceeded the specified exemption amount. (A copy of this letter appears on the next page.) Now, let me add this: Unless you work for the federal government and/or live in a federal area, then, you, like us, are not liable to file an individual INCOME tax return. Read on, and you will learn truths which will anger you but, ultimately, set you free.

The fundamental truth is that the federal United States Government has made asses out of all of us. More than asses, it has made us slaves. We the People have been voluntarily turning over up to 50% or more of our WAGES—not because we owe it, but because they SAY we do. Would you have believed that our government was not to be trusted?

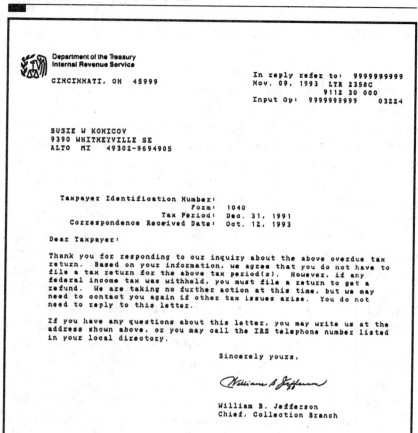

Department of the Treasury
Internal Revenue Service

CINCINNATI, OH 45999

In reply refer to: 9999999999
Nov. 09, 1993 LTR 2358C
9112 30 000
Input Op: 9999999999 03224

SUSIE W KONICOV
9390 WHITNEYVILLE SE
ALTO MI 49302-9694905

Taxpayer Identification Number:
Form: 1040
Tax Period: Dec. 31, 1991
Correspondence Received Date: Oct. 12, 1993

Dear Taxpayer:

Thank you for responding to our inquiry about the above overdue tax return. Based on your information, we agree that you do not have to file a tax return for the above tax period(s). However, if any federal income tax was withheld, you must file a return to get a refund. We are taking no further action at this time, but we may need to contact you again if other tax issues arise. You do not need to reply to this letter.

If you have any questions about this letter, you may write us at the address shown above, or you may call the IRS telephone number listed in your local directory.

Sincerely yours,

William B. Jefferson
Chief, Collection Branch

HAVE YOU READ
A GOOD CONSTITUTION LATELY?

When was the last time that you read the Constitution and the Bill of Rights? I don't remember ever reading them in school, but, lately, I have read and re-read them until there are some portions that I can recite from memory.

The men who founded this country did so by creating three documents: the Declaration of Independence, the Constitution, and the Bill of Rights. They placed within these documents elements which were intended to protect future generations from the insane perversion of governmental power.

When you read over these documents, you come to the inescapable conclusion that what the Founding Fathers freed themselves from has, again, re-created itself in these United States. You will be led to understand that the United States Government is doing precisely the same thing to We the People that the English Government did to the colonists. The only difference, now, is that We the People do not have to fight for our rights. We only need to stand up for them. We only need to acknowledge the Constitution as the supreme law of the land and demand that our public employees obey the Constitution.

The Constitution is a contract which our employees have sworn "to uphold and defend." We the People are obligated to hold our employees accountable for violations of their employment contract. A violation of the supreme law of the land, the Constitution, is TREASON.

THE CONSTITUTION IS THE SUPREME LAW OF THE LAND

"This Constitution, and the Laws of the United States which shall be made in Pursuance thereof; and all Treaties made, or which shall be made, under the Authority of the United States, shall be the supreme Law of the Land; and the Judges in every State shall be bound thereby, any Thing in the Constitution or Laws of any State to the Contrary notwithstanding."

Article VI

WHICH UNITED STATES ARE WE TALKING ABOUT?

Before I gained this knowledge, I had no idea that the term "united States" had three separate and distinct meanings. To me, there was no distinction. Because I didn't understand the differences, I was conned into paying federal income tax. It is very important that you understand the three different ways that the term "united States" is used. Understanding them will help you to free yourself legally from the INCOME tax.

"The term 'united States' may be used in any one of several senses. It may be merely the name of a sovereign occupying the position analogous to that of other sovereigns in the family of nations. It may designate the territory over which the sovereignty of the United States extends. Or it may be the collective name of the States,... united by and under the Constitution."

Hooven & Allison Co. v Evatt, 324 U.S. 652; 65 S. Ct. 870; 89 L. Ed. 1252 (1945)

You and I live in a sovereign state or country to the "federal United States." If we substituted the words "Mexican Government," it would be easier for most of us to understand. I won't do that. Instead, I will use the term "federal United States." For the purposes of individual taxation, the federal United States is a foreign country. It is located in Washington D.C. and has limited powers. These powers are spelled out in the Constitution, which grants to the federal United States the following right:

"To exercise exclusive Legislation in all Cases whatsoever, over such District (not exceeding ten Miles square) as may, by Cession of Particular States, and the Acceptance of Congress, become the Seat of the Government of the United States, and to exercise like Authority over all Places purchased by the Consent of the Legislature of the State in which the Same shall be, for the Erection of Forts, Magazines, Arsenals, dock-Yards, and other needful Buildings,—And

To make all Laws which shall be necessary and proper for carrying into Execution the foregoing Powers, and all other Powers vested by the Constitution in the Government of the United States, or in any Department or Office thereof."

Article I, Section 8

There is no question that, if you live in the federal United States, you are subject to its laws. And, if these laws say that it can tax its citizen subjects, then you can legally be taxed. But, for us living outside of the federal United States, the Constitution limited the power of the federal United States to tax us directly.

WHAT IS A DIRECT TAX?

The Constitution says that the federal United States has no authority to tax us directly. It does, however, recognize that situations may arise where the federal United States may need to raise money from the citizens of the individual states. Therefore, it does allow for the federal United States to pass the tax on to the individual states for collection. It authorizes this when it states in Article I, Section 2:

"Representatives and direct Taxes shall be apportioned among the several States which may be included within this Union, according to their respective Numbers..."

The next time the Constitution talks about direct taxes is in Article I, Section 9, when it says:

"No Capitation, or other direct tax shall be laid, unless in Proportion to the Census or Enumeration herein before directed to be taken."

According to the Constitution, the federal United States has no authority to tax you directly. It has no more power to do that than the Mexican Government has. The federal United States Government gets away with it because We the People allow it to.

THE SIXTEENTH AMENDMENT

The I.R.S. loves the Sixteenth Amendment. If you were to call them and ask them where they get the authority to tax you directly, they would point to the Sixteenth Amendment. Here is what the amendment says:

"The Congress shall have power to lay and collect taxes on INCOMES, from whatever source derived, without apportionment among the several States, and without regard to any census or enumeration." [emphasis added]

At first reading, it would appear that this amendment has stripped away the Constitutional provisions prohibiting direct taxation. But do not assume that the federal United States is now free to reach directly into your pocket and tax your wages directly because that is not so. The amendment is talking about INCOME. You are assuming that you have INCOME.

INCOME V. WAGES

INCOME is not defined in the Internal Revenue Code. Congress has never defined INCOME. The courts have defined INCOME as accounting profit or gain.

"There is a clear distinction between 'profit' and 'wages,' or compensation for labor. 'Compensation for labor' (wages) cannot be regarded as profit within the meaning of the law. The word 'profit', as ordinarily used, means the gain made upon any business or investment—a different thing altogether from the mere compensation for labor."

Oliver v Halstead
196 Va. 992; 86 S.E. 2d 858 (1955)

There are numerous court cases which prove that wages are not taxable. The following legal presentation was provided by Al Carter of the American Institute for the Republic in Provo, Utah. Al received the information from an anonymous source in the I.R.S.

TAX LAW ORIGINS AND AUTHORITY

Congress has had the power to lay and collect income taxes from the time of the adoption of the Constitution. See Brushaber v Union Pacific R.R. Co., 240 U.S. 1; 36 S.Ct. 236; 60 L. Ed. 493 (1916). This power was subject to the requirement that direct taxes be apportioned among the several states according to population. See Pollock v Farmers Loan and Trust Co., 157 U.S. 429; 15 S.Ct. 673; 39 L. Ed. 821 (1895). The adoption of the Sixteenth Amendment to the Constitution, effective Feb. 25, 1913, gave Congress the power to:

"lay and collect taxes on income, from whatever source derived, without apportionment among the several States, and without regard to any census or enumeration."

Note: See Evans v Gore, 253 U.S. 245; 40 S.Ct. 550; 64 L. Ed. 887 (1920), and Kasey v C.I.R., 457 F. 2d 369 (CA9, 1972).

It did not limit or expand the power of Congress to tax under the Constitutional provisions authorizing Congress to lay and collect taxes. Instead, it merely provided for the taxation of income without apportionment. See Brushaber decision, Simmons v U.S., 308 F. 2d 160 (CA4, 1962), and Pledger v C.I.R., 641 F. 2d 287 (CA5, 1981); Certiorari denied 454 U.S. 964.

The Brushaber court ruled that the Sixteenth Amendment separated the source (capital) from the income (profit), permitting the collection of indirect (excise) taxes on income but leaving the source (wages, salary, compensation, fees for service, first-time commissions, and capital) untouched and free of tax. If these things were to be taxed, it could only be construed as a direct tax, that would, unquestionably, be in violation of the Constitution, making the entire tax on income void.

There still remains the question as to what is constitutionally allowable as "income" which can be taxed, as Congress is not Constitutionally free to define "income" in any way it chooses. See Simpson v U.S., 423 F. Supp. 720 (S.D. IA, 1976), which was reversed on other grounds, and Prescott v Commissioner of Internal Revenue, 561 F. 2d 1287 (CA8,1977). Further, the labels used do not determine the extent of the taxing power. See Richardson v U.S., 294 F. 2d 593 (CA6, 1961); Certiorari denied 360 U.S. 802.

To reiterate, the tax authorized under the original U.S. Constitution has not changed except to separate the source of "income" from the income, itself, permitting the collection of an indirect (excise) tax on income by leaving the source (wages, salaries, fees for service, and first-time commissions) free of tax, (Brushaber supra), despite how some politicians interpret the Sixteenth Amendment.

Note: The Brushaber court referred to an earlier case, see Pollock decision, which declared the Income Tax Act of 1894 unconstitutional, as its effect would have been to leave the burden of the tax to be born by professions, trades, employments, or vocations. In that way, what was intended as a tax on capital would remain, in substance, a tax on occupations and labor. This result, the court held, could NOT have been contemplated by Congress.

Note: There are also questions as to both the ratification and the constitutionality of the Sixteenth Amendment. But neither has been ruled on by the U.S. Supreme Court, so why clutter up a good defense?

Since the general term "income" is not defined in the Internal Revenue Code per U.S. v Ballard, 535 F. 2d 400 (CA8, 1976), the U.S. Supreme Court has ruled that Congress may not, by any definition it may adopt, conclude the matter, since it cannot by legislation alter the Constitution, from which alone it derives that its power can be lawfully exercised. See Eisner v Macomber, 252 U.S. 189; 40 S.Ct. 189; 64 L. Ed. 521 (1920).

Since the Rules contained in the I.R.S. Manual, even if codified in the code of Federal Regulations, do not have the force and effect of law, (U.S. v Horne, 714 F. 2d 207 (CA1, 1983)), and since the power to promulgate regulations does not include the power to broaden or narrow what Congress intended, (Abbot, Proctor & Paine v U.S., 344 F. 2d 333 (Ct. of Cl., 1965)), and regulations cannot do what Congress, itself, is without power to do, they must conform to the Constitution. See C.I.R. v Van Vorst, 59 F. 2d 677, 680 (CA9, 1932).

Since the ultimate appellate court is the U.S. Supreme Court, we must look to them for a definite answer to the question of conformance and affirmation of our little secret that wages are not classified as income, which can be taxed.

The Court has recognized that ... *"it becomes essential to distinguish between what is, and what is not, income"* ... (See Eisner decision) and determined that ... *"income as used in the statute should be given a meaning so as not to include everything that comes in. The true function of the words 'gains' and 'profits' is to limit the meaning of the word 'income.'"*

See So. Pacific v Lowe, 238 F. 2d 847 (CA2, 1917). The Court also determined that ...

"[T]he definition of income approved by the Court is: The gain derived from capital, from labor, or from both combined, provided it be understood to include profits gained through sale or conversion of capital assets."

Eisner decision

"Income within the meaning of the Sixteenth Amendment and the Revenue Act means gain ... and, in such connection, gain means profit ... proceeding from property severed from capital, however invested or employed and coming in, received or drawn by the taxpayer for his separate use, benefit and disposal."

Staples v U.S., 21 F. Supp. 737 (D.C., 1937)

In the case of Lucas v Earl, 281 U.S. 111; 50 S.Ct. 241; 74 L. Ed. 731 (1930), the U.S. Supreme Court stated unambiguously that ...

"The claim that salaries, wages, and compensation for personal services are to be taxed as an entirety and therefore must be returned by the individual who has performed the services which produce the gain is without support, either in the language of the Act or in the decisions of the courts construing it. Not only this, but it is directly opposed to provisions of the Act and to regulations of the U.S. Treasury Department, which either prescribes or permits that compensation for personal services not be taxed as an entirety and not be returned by the individual performing the services. It is to be noted that, by the language of the Act, it is not salaries, wages, or compensation for personal services that are to be included in gains, profits, and income derived from salaries, wages or compensation for personal service."

The Court ruled similarly in Goodrich v Edwards, 255 U.S. 527; 41 S.Ct. 390; 65 L. Ed. 758 (1921). And, in 1969, the Court ruled in Connor v U.S., 303 F. Supp. 1187 (S.D. TX, 1969), that ...

"[W]hatever may constitute income, therefore, must have the essential feature of gain to the recipient. This was true when the Sixteenth Amendment became effective, it was true at the time of

Eisner v Macomber, supra, it was true under Section 22(a) of the Internal Revenue Code of 1938, and it is likewise true under Section 61(a) of the Internal Revenue Code of 1954. If there is not gain, there is not income...Congress has taxed INCOME not compensation."

"...one does not derive income by rendering services and charging for them."

Edwards v Keith, 224 F. 585 (D.C.); 231 F. 110 (CA4, 1916)

Even at the State level, we find courts following the lead of the U.S. Supreme Court:

"There is a clear distinction between profit and wages, or compensation for labor. Compensation for labor cannot be regarded as profit within the meaning of the law."

Oliver decision

"[R]easonable compensation for labor or services rendered is not profit."

Lauderdale Cemetary Assoc. v Matthews,
354 Pa 239; 47 A. 2d 277 (1946)

The above cases are not the undisputable law with respect to what is or is not income. However, we find that the word "income" is not defined as all monies that come into the possession of an individual. "Income" is defined as profit or gain from the money one takes in, such as interest, stock dividends, or profit from an employee's labor. "Income" is not defined as profit or gain from an individual's wages, which are compensation for his labor. This means that the average person in America, who has no large investments or riches upon which he receives interest or dividends in excess of the allowable amount, has an insufficient amount of income to be required to file a tax return.

RETURN TO CAESAR
WHAT IS CAESAR'S

If you work for Caesar and/or live in Caesar's home, then you are liable to Caesar. You owe something to Caesar. Likewise, if you work for the federal United States Government and/or live in a territory which is under its control, then you are liable to the federal United States Government. If this is your situation, then you must return a portion of what you have gained by either working for the federal government or living in a federal area to the federal government.

Most of us do not fall into this category. Therefore, we are paying taxes under what the Internal Revenue Service calls voluntary compliance. We must be paying taxes voluntarily because there is no law which requires us to file or pay individual income taxes. You can verify this yourself by calling the Internal Revenue Service at 1-800- 829-1040 and asking them, "What law requires me to file an income tax return?" If the I.R.S. tells you that the law is the Sixteenth Amendment, you know from what you have read in "The Story of Taxes" that the Sixteenth Amendment grants Congress the authority to tax income and that what you receive as compensation for your labor is wages.

However, if the agent tells you that the I.R.S.'s authority to tax you comes from the Internal Revenue Code, (Title 26), then you have now entered into a whole new ballgame. The keys to understanding the rules of this new game are simple: Never take anything at face value, and question everything. If the Internal Revenue Code tells you that there are seven days in a week, don't believe it. You may know that there are seven days in a week. But what about the seven nights? And what about the time in between day and night? The I.R.S. has its own set of rules and applies entirely different meanings to the everyday words that you and I use. You will come to understand what I mean in a few minutes.

In order to successfully navigate the I.R.S. maze, you must

keep a couple of additional things in mind. First, this great country was founded by a group of tax protesters. In creating this country, they bequeathed to us a system of government which was free from direct taxation. The three documents that created this country—the Declaration of Independence, the Constitution, and the Bill of Rights (the first ten amendments to the Constitution)—make it practically impossible for the federal United States Government to tax We the People directly. Second, the federal United States Government has absolute control over its federal areas and can do just about anything it chooses within those areas because it is Caesar. Those who work for the federal United States Government and/or live in a federal area are subjects of the federal United States Government.

For these individuals, the Internal Revenue Code is law. But for the rest of us, it has no particular meaning. That is why the I.R.S. keeps telling us that our income tax system is voluntary. In an article which appeared in a special edition to *The New York Times* in March of 1994, the Commissioner of the Internal Revenue Service, Ms. Margaret Milner Richardson, made the point that our income tax system is voluntary. (See next page.)

HOW DID I VOLUNTEER TO PAY TAXES?

By now you know that there is no law which makes you liable to file or pay federal income taxes. But I'm sure that you are wondering what you did to get yourself into this mess. When you were hired, chances are that your employer handed you a stack of papers. Among those papers were one or more documents which authorized your employer to deduct a certain amount from your paycheck and send it to the federal United States Government.

Until you signed these forms, your employment contract was only with your employer. Your contract called for a certain amount of work for a certain amount of pay, and the government had no business in your business unless you were engaged in an activity that made you liable for a tax imposed by the federal United States

Government (a revenue-taxable activity). But neither you nor your employer knew that. Once you signed those documents, the government became a third party to your employment agreement. You agreed to become a taxpayer, and your employer agreed to collect the tax and forward it to the I.R.S.

Margaret Milner Richardson, Washington tax lawyer and Southern Democratic loyalist, sees her place as President Clinton's Internal Revenue Commissioner as "the biggest fund-raising job there is."

Washington at Work

A Tax Lawyer Now Atop the I.R.S.
MAR 3 0 1994

By ROBERT D. HERSHEY JR.

Special to the New York Times

WASHINGTON, March 29 — A year ago, just after President Clinton announced her nomination as Commissioner of Internal Revenue, Margaret Milner Richardson was toasted at lunch by friends, all female tax lawyers. Someone mentioned her legendary success as a fund-raiser for political causes and charities.

"Well, I think I'm now going into the biggest fund-raising job there is," responded the Vassar graduate, originally from Waco, Tex., who took a leave of absence from her Washing-ton law firm to work in Mr. Clinton's campaign. "And this time," she added, thinking of the agency's 115,000 employees and vast legal powers, "I won't even have to use my Rolodex."

In the throes of her first filing season, which officials say has produced few problems besides a slower-than-usual flow of returns because of the winter's snow and ice, Mrs. Richardson is charged with one of the Government's formidable challenges.

Her mission is to oversee the continuing transformation of an agency whose structure evolved in the early 50's, and whose computers date from the 1960's, into a center efficient enough to collect $1 trillion a year in

taxes as well as to try to get some of the estimated $150 billion that slips through the Treasury's hands.

"We realize that for our voluntary income tax system to survive, and for us to accomplish our mission, we need to change the way we do business," Mrs. Richardson said recently, adding she was shocked to learn that 10 million individuals and businesses file no returns.

She promised to "listen to our customers" who have become accustomed to instant account service by credit-card companies and others in

Continued on Page D16

WHY ME?
SECTION 3402(a), THAT'S WHY!

Your employer gave you those documents because he believed, as you did, that paying income tax was the law. Rarely would an employer ask his accountant or any legal authority what law gave him the authority to withhold money from your paycheck. But if he would have, he would have been directed to Internal Revenue Code Section 3402(a). Let's take a look at the pertinent part of this section:

(a) Requirement of withholding.

(1) In general. Except as otherwise provided in this section, every employer making payment of wages shall deduct and withhold upon such wages a tax... .

At first reading, it would appear that you work for your employer and that, according to the code, your employer is required to withhold taxes from your paycheck. But remember what I told you earlier about the Internal Revenue Code. The code is only law

29

if you are a person made liable for income taxes. However, you can *voluntarily* make yourself liable. And, in the game of taxes, that is exactly what you have done. You have made yourself liable.

Let me prove to you that the income tax system is voluntary by approaching the withholding of taxes from the position of your employer. If there were a law which required your employer to withhold money from your paycheck and forward it to the I.R.S., then your employer would be working for the government. And, if the government required your employer to work for it without payment, then your employer would be a slave to the government. (A slave is a person whose time is controlled by another person.) But your employer is not a slave to the government because of the wording of the code.

The code is carefully worded in order to insure that no one could successfully challenge the I.R.S. on the slavery issue. The code uses the words "shall deduct and withhold." This is legal foreplay. When the government uses the word "shall," it means "may"— "may" as in "you may not have to do this because it is voluntary."

There is only one employer who "shall deduct and withhold" without being a slave. And that employer is the federal United States Government. Proof positive that the employer referred to in 3402(a) is the federal government is found by looking up the definition of "employee" in the code.

Section 3401(c). Employee.

For purposes of this chapter, the term "employee" includes an officer, employee, or elected official of the United States, a State, or any political subdivision thereof, or the District of Columbia, or any agency or instrumentality of any one or more of the foregoing.

If we know that the employee in 3401(c) works for the government and that you work for an employer other than the federal government, then we know that your employer is not the employer referred to in 3402(a). Therefore, since your employer is not being paid for what he is doing for the government and he is not a slave, he is volunteering.

By now you are probably asking yourself how so many people could have been fooled for so long. The answer is that We the People have been enslaved by fear and ignorance. It has been said that ignorance of the law is no defense. It may not be a defense, but it is the reason. We have been taught to believe in and trust our government. While it is a well-known fact that some common words have entirely different meanings in law (or, in this case, the Internal Revenue Code Book), when that discrepancy in meaning is used to enslave us, I believe that it is time for change. You can begin any time you want, and you can begin by volunteering out of the voluntary income tax system.

A State?

When you read through Section 3401(c), you noticed that the words "United States" were followed by the words "a State." As you may have guessed, when the I.R.S. uses the words "a State," it has something very specific in mind.

Section 7701(a)(10):

(a) When used in this title, where not otherwise distinctly expressed or manifestly incompatible with the intent thereof-

(10) State. The term 'State' shall be construed to include the District of Columbia, where such construction is necessary to carry out provisions of this title.

If you thought that you lived in "a state" (as those words are commonly understood), then you were right. But the words "a State" mean something entirely different to the I.R.S. The District of Columbia, (Washington D.C.), is the home of the federal United States Government. And, if you live in that state, then the Internal Revenue Code is law for you.

Free at Last, Almost

There is another section of the Internal Revenue Code that frees We the People from the tax man. That section is 3402(n). This section exempts everyone but federal government employees, federal subjects, and those who have made themselves liable for filing and paying federal income taxes.

Section 3402(n). Employees incurring no income tax liability.

Notwithstanding any other provision of this section, an employer shall not be required to deduct and withhold any tax under this chapter upon a payment of wages to an employee if there is in effect with respect to such payment a withholding exemption certificate ... furnished to the employer by the employee certifying that the employee-

(1) incurred no liability for income tax imposed under subtitle A for his preceding taxable year, and

(2) anticipates that he will incur no liability for income tax imposed under subtitle A for his current taxable year.

Only federal employees, federal subjects, or people who make themselves liable are subject to tax under the Internal Revenue Code. In order to secure an exempt status, an employee must file a certificate with his employer which states his exemption.

CONCLUSION

There is no law that requires you to file an individual income tax return, unless you work for the federal government, live in a federal area, or are engaged in a revenue-taxable activity. Your employer is sending your money to the federal United States Government because you told him to. Finally, your employer is doing work for the federal government on a voluntary basis.

If you should decide to change your contractual agreement with your employer, remember this: You have a contract which calls for a certain amount of work for a certain amount of pay. If you decide to stop sending your money to the government, then that is your business. If your employer continues to send your money to the government after you have submitted the proper documentation, then you can sue him for breach of contract.

DIRECT & INDIRECT TAXES & THE 16TH AMENDMENT

In "The Story of Taxes," I quoted from the Constitution and from Supreme Court decisions to prove that what you earn for your labor is a wage and that your wages are not taxable. I may have left a few loose ends and, perhaps, a few questions in your mind that I would like to clear up now.

Our Constitution speaks of two types of taxes, direct and indirect. To understand the differences between these two types of taxes is to understand the distinction between wages and income. Remember that the Supreme Court has ruled that wages are not taxable, whereas income is taxable. The Sixteenth Amendment plays a very important role in clarifying the distinction between direct and indirect taxes, as you will see shortly.

DIRECT TAXES

Direct taxes are taxes which are imposed on people and property. A direct tax on a person is called a capitation tax. Here is what the Constitution says about the federal United States Government's ability to levy and collect capitation and other direct taxes:

"No Capitation, or other direct tax shall be laid, unless in Proportion to the Census or Enumeration herein before directed to be taken."

(Article I, Section 9, Clause 4)

A tax on you, or a capitation tax, is just about as direct as you can get. Head taxes are grossly unfair. Having the same level of taxation imposed upon everyone without consideration of his or her ability to pay forces a person with modest means to work more hours to pay the tax than a person with greater means.

For example, suppose that the government imposed a head

tax of $100 on every person. If you earned $10 per hour, you would have to work ten hours to pay the tax. A person earning $100 an hour would only have to work one hour. You would be forced into working nine more hours to pay the same tax. A capitation tax would be unconstitutional because it would treat us unequally.

The Declaration of Independence is clear on the issue of equality—all people are to be treated equally.

"We hold these truths to be self-evident, that all men are created equal, ... "

Because of this clause, the codes, regulations, and laws which are created by government on all levels must be equally applied.

The Constitution does allow the federal government to collect a direct tax provided that it is "in Proportion to the Census or Enumeration herein before directed to be taken." In order to understand what the Constitution is referring to by "Census or Enumeration," we need to refer back to Article I, Section 2, Clause 3:

"Representatives and direct Taxes shall be apportioned among the several States which may be included within this Union, according to their respective Numbers [which shall be determined by adding to the whole Number of free persons, including those bound to Service for a Term of Years, and excluding Indians not taxed, three-fifths of all other Persons]. "

If the federal United States Government were to tax We the People directly, it would have to take these two steps. First, it would have to determine how much money it needs. And, second, it would have to divide that amount among the states in proportion to their census or enumeration. The states would then collect the money from We the People and transfer it to the federal government.

Because of constitutional safeguards, it is practically impossible for the federal United States Government to tax We the People directly. Our Founding Fathers planned it that way. They had just fought a war for their freedom with England, the strongest country in the world. They had seen how government for the few could be used to enslave the many. They were not going to re-create a system of government which would enslave free men as they had been enslaved. It was their intention to create a small, central government which was limited in its authority, power, and responsibilities. They believed that limiting the government's ability to raise revenue would ensure a small federal government— one confined to a ten-mile enclave called the District of Columbia.

Our Founding Fathers knew that most governments, over time, become enemies of We the People. To protect us from the very government that they were creating was their gravest challenge.

Fundamental to protecting the people from the government was insuring that We the People had a stake in something which we could call our own. Our Founding Fathers believed that, if the people owned property, then they would defend that property, even against their own government.

Our Founding Fathers believed that you had a right to own property and that your property rights began with your labor. It is from your labor that all of your property flows. If you cannot own and control your own labor, then you can never own and control any other form of property. Your right to own property is sacred and inviolable.

The Founding Fathers believed that the right to work and the right to keep what one earns from his labor comes from God. The Declaration of Independence, talking about rights, affirms that all rights come from God:

"We hold these truths to be self-evident, that all men are created equal, that they are endowed by their Creator with certain unalienable Rights, that among these are Life, Liberty and the pursuit of Happiness."

No tax can be imposed upon a God-given right—EVER!

You cannot give your rights away, nor can they be taken from you. But you can pretend that you have given them away or that they have been taken from you. Governments would like you to believe that rights come from them in the form of "civil rights," or "privileges." The government would like you to believe that you are obligated to pay a tax for the right to work. Our Founding Fathers revolted when England attempted to impose a tax of just 1% on them. Today, all of the taxes imposed on you, taken together, consume more than 70% of your wages.

For a long time I believed in the government's insanity. I believed that they had the right to tax my wages. But then I began to awaken. Since that time, I have been taking the hands of government out of my pockets. I legally stopped paying federal, state, and Social Security taxes. My question to you is this: How long will it be before you wake up?

INDIRECT TAXES

"The Congress shall have Power to lay and collect Taxes, Duties, Imposts and Excises, to pay the Debts and provide for the common Defence and general Welfare of the United States; but all Duties, Imposts and Excises shall be uniform throughout the United States."

(U.S. Constitution, Article I, Section 8, Clause 1)

Duties and imposts are taxes on the importation and exportation of products. Whereas Excise taxes ...

"... are taxes laid upon the manufacture, sale or consumption of commodities within the country, upon license to pursue certain occupations and upon corporate privileges; the requirement to pay such taxes involves the exercise of a privilege."

Flint v Stone Tracy Co., 220 U.S. 107 (1911)

Indirect taxes are always imposed upon an activity or event which is taxable for revenue purposes. An indirect tax must be applied uniformly, meaning that the same percentage must be applied everywhere in the country. It is a tax on an activity, never a tax which is directly upon persons, property, or products. You pay, literally, hundreds of indirect taxes. At all times and under all conditions, excise taxes are collected from revenue-taxable activities.

The most common products which have excise taxes attached to them are alcohol, tobacco, and firearms. The government taxes these products because of the negative effect which their comsumption or use has upon society. Obviously, society does pay a big price due to the effects of alcohol, tobacco, and firearms.

That is why some people refer to an excise tax as a "sin" tax.

There are several characteristics which all excise taxes have in common. Generally, if you do not want to pay an excise tax, then you simply avoid buying that particular product. But, if you do buy the product, then you do so of your own free will.

A second characteristic of excise taxes is that they are passed along from the manufacturer to the final user. In the case of alcohol, tobacco, and firearm products, the tax is placed on the manufacturer of the product and passed from the manufacturer to the wholesaler, then the distributor, then the retailer, and, finally, on to the consumer.

Before I began studying the tax issue, I didn't have a clue as to the difference between direct and indirect taxes. Yet, it is understanding the difference between them that opened the door wide and freed me from the 1040 U.S. Individual Income Tax Return.

ENTER THE
SIXTEENTH AMENDMENT

When people call or write the I.R.S. for information about the law that requires them to file an income tax return, I.R.S. agents often say that their taxing authority comes from the Sixteenth Amendment because the Sixteenth Amendment gives Congress the right to tax income. But this is only partly true because Congress has always had the right to tax income.

What the I.R.S. is hoping that you and their employees will never find out is that the words "income" and "wages" have entirely different legal meanings. The I.R.S. is hoping against hope that you will not learn that what you earn from your labor is wages and, simply put, that wages are your property and that they cannot be taxed directly by the federal government. The government is afraid that We the People will catch them in a lie. The I.R.S. is hoping that their employees will never find out the truth so that they can keep on lying with a straight face.

This time when you read the Sixteenth Amendment, read it knowing that it is making a distinction between a direct and an

indirect tax. And know that the word "income" tells you that income taxes are indirect, excise taxes which ...

*"... are taxes laid upon the manufacture, sale or consumption
of commodities within the country, upon license to pursue certain
occupations and upon corporate privileges; the requirement to
pay such taxes involves the exercise of a privilege."*

Flint v Stone Tracy Co., supra

THE SIXTEENTH AMENDMENT

*"The Congress shall have power to lay and collect taxes on
incomes, from whatever source derived, without apportionment
among the several States, and without regard to any census or
enumeration."*

Now that you know that the amendment is referring to indirect taxes, you have every right to be angry. Who among us knew
that income is taxable but that wages are not? There is only one
reason why something this important is not taught in the schools.
Obviously, our slave masters did not want us to know.

The Sixteenth Amendment adds nothing to the Constitution,
nor does it change anything in the Constitution. It has no imple-
menting clause—nothing which grants Congress the authority to
make a law in order to implement the amendment. Therefore, you
know that the amendment was not intended to change anything
in the Constitution. It clarified what had previously been said.

RATIFIED OR NOT, IT MAKES NO DIFFERENCE!

Much has been written proving that the Sixteenth Amendment
was never properly ratified. The proof was found by Bill Benson
and documented in a two-volume work entitled, *The Law That
Never Was.*

I have talked to Bill Benson on several occasions. I know him
to be a man committed to his truth. I believe him when he says
that the Sixteenth Amendment was never properly ratified. But,

ratified or not, it makes no difference. The Supreme Court has ruled in the Brushaber case that the amendment did not change the Constitution, but rather clarified the distinction between direct and indirect taxes. Because the Brushaber case is so important, I have included it in this book. No one can be considered knowledgeable in the subject of taxes unless he has an understanding of this case.

THE PROOF

Before we leave this chapter, let's pause for a moment and focus on the decision of the Supreme Court in Fisher v Redfield, 292 P 2d 813; (1930) cert. d'ned 284 U.S. 617; 52 S.Ct. 6; ____ L. Ed. _____ (1931).

"The individual, unlike the corporation, cannot be taxed for the mere privilege of existing. The corporation is an artificial entity which owes its existence and charter powers to the state; but the individuals' right to own property are natural rights for the enjoyment of which an excise cannot be imposed..."

IF FREEDOM CALLS

First change yourself, then change the world.

THREE BLIND MICE

After more than a year of chiding people to call the I.R.S. for the answer to the question, "What law makes me liable to file an individual income tax return?", I can say that the "answer" most often given is Internal Revenue Code sections 6001, 6011, and 6012. I am going to call these three code sections the three blind mice because, if you follow them, they will lead you nowhere near the answer to the question. However, by *not* answering the question, the I.R.S. *does* answer the question.

The three blind mice are featured both in the instruction booklet for the 1040 and in Notice 609. But nowhere is the deception of our government more present and less evident than in Notice 609. Take a few minutes to read over Notice 609 (next page) very carefully. The ugliness begins in the first sentence when it states:

"The Privacy Act of 1974 says that when we ask you for information, we must first tell you our legal right to ask for the information, why we are asking for it, and how it will be used."

The key word in this quotation is "ask." If I came up to you and asked you for something, you could simply say "no." But was there ever a time when the I.R.S. asked for something and the person being asked was aware that he had a right to say "no?" If the I.R.S. asks you for something, you can bet your last nickel that they have no legal right to obtain that information. But if the I.R.S. gets you to voluntarily turn the information over to them in response to their request, then they haven't done anything illegal.

The reason that the I.R.S. plays this game of "asking" for information as opposed to demanding information is this: You have a right to say "no." You have rights granted to you by your Creator. And, because these rights come from your Creator, the government cannot take them away. But, if the government can deceive or intimidate you into giving up your God-given rights, then, in the eyes of the law, it has done nothing wrong. Some of your God-given rights are set forth in the Bill of Rights. At this time, let's give

**Department of the Treasury
Internal Revenue Service**

Notice 609

(Revised April 1992)

Privacy Act Notice

The Privacy Act of 1974 says that when we ask you for information, we must first tell you our legal right to ask for the information, why we are asking for it, and how it will be used. We must also tell you what could happen if you do not provide it and whether or not you must respond under the law.

This notice applies to tax returns and any papers filed with them. It also applies to any questions we need to ask you so we can complete, correct, or process your return; figure your tax; and collect tax, interest, or penalties.

Our legal right to ask for information is Internal Revenue Code sections 6001, 6011, and 6012(a) and their regulations. They say that you must file a return or statement with us for any tax you are liable for. Your response is mandatory under these sections.

Code section 6109 and its regulations say that you must show your social security number on what you file. You must also fill in all parts of the tax form that apply to you. This is so we know who you are, and can process your return and papers. You do not have to check the boxes for the Presidential Election Campaign Fund.

We ask for tax return information to carry out the U.S. tax laws. We need it to figure and collect the right amount of tax.

We may give the information to the Department of Justice and to other Federal agencies, as provided by law. We may also give it to cities, states, the District of Columbia, and U.S. commonwealths or possessions to carry out their tax laws. And we may give it to certain foreign governments under tax treaties they have with the United States.

Cat. No. 45963A

particular attention to the Fourth and Fifth Amendments:

Article IV - "The right of the people to be secure in their persons, houses, papers, and effects, against unreasonable searches and seizures, shall not be violated, and no Warrants shall issue, but upon probable cause, supported by Oath or Affirmation, and particularly describing the place to be searched, and the persons or things to be seized."

Article V - "No person shall...be compelled in any criminal case to be a witness against himself, nor be deprived of life, liberty, or property, without due process of law; nor shall private property be taken for public use, without just compensation."

The I.R.S. uses the word "ask" because they know the law. Individuals at the very top levels of the I.R.S. know that the Constitution protects you. They know that you have the right to say no. Maybe not every I.R.S. employee knows this, but the ones at the top do. The following appears in the I.R.S.'s own *Handbook for Special Agents* under Section 343.12 - Constitutional Law:

"The privilege against self-incrimination does not permit a taxpayer to refuse to obey a summons issued under IRC 7602 or a court order directing his/her appearance. He/she is required to appear and cannot use the Fifth Amendment as an excuse for failure to do so, although he/she may exercise it in connection with specific questions. (Landy v U.S.) He/she cannot refuse to bring his/her records, but may decline to submit them for inspection on constitutional grounds. In the Vader case, the government moved to hold a taxpayer in contempt of court for refusal to obey a court order to produce his/her books and records. Vader refused to submit them for inspection by the government, basing his refusal on the Fifth Amendment. The court denied the government's motion to hold Vader in contempt, adding that disclosure of his assets would provide a starting point for a tax evasion case."

The I.R.S. knows the law. They also know that the vast majority of We the People do not. The I.R.S. knows that most of us, out of fear and ignorance, will turn anything over to them that they ask for.

THE CONSTITUTION, THE COURTS, AND THE I.R.S.

The federal courts have consistently and specifically upheld the Constitution and the Bill of Rights in matters of taxation. It has been We the People who have not stood up to authority. There is no one to blame. We are responsible. And, unless and until we stand up to the government and to the I.R.S., we will remain slaves of the system.

Many people are intimidated by the I.R.S, but not William T. Conklin. He has been in the face of the I.R.S. for years. In the mid-'80s, he began advertising a reward of $50,000 to anyone who could show him:

1.   The statute in the Internal Revenue Code that made him liable to pay income tax, and

2.   How he could file a 1040 tax return without waiving his Fifth Amendment rights.

In November of 1994 in Colorado, the Tenth Circuit Court of Appeals affirmed the U.S. District Court's opinion in the case of William T. Conklin v United States (Civil Action No. 89N1514 filed on May 2, 1994). In a decision which Paul Harvey reported on his national radio program, the court ruled that filing a tax return is not required because, if it were, it would compel the individual to give testimony against himself. This decision expanded the U.S. Supreme Court decision in Garner v United States, 424 U.S. 648; 96 S.Ct. 1178; 47 L. Ed. 2d 370 (1976), in which the court ruled that the information contained on a tax return constitutes "compelled testimonial communication." The Garner court stated:

"The information revealed in the preparation and filing of an income tax return is, for purposes of Fifth Amendment analysis, the testimony of a witness."

The Conklin case is further supported by an earlier case, United States v Doe, 465 U.S. 605; 104 S.Ct. 1237; 79 L. Ed. 2d 552 (1984). In the Doe case, the court ruled that the Fifth Amendment protection covers both written and oral testimony. But it also ruled that, if you sign a 1040 tax return under penalty of perjury, then you have given up your rights and the information you voluntarily gave may, can, and shall be used against you.

Remember that the Fifth Amendment protects you from being a witness against yourself. That is one of the primary reasons why filing a tax return is not required. You simply cannot be required to be a witness against yourself.

Here's what the Supreme Court has said regarding our Fourth Amendment rights:

"It does not require the actual entry upon premises and search for a seizure of papers to constitute an unreasonable search and seizure within the meaning of the Fourth Amendment. The compulsory production of a party's books and records, to be used against himself or his property in a criminal or penal proceeding, or a forfeiture, is within the spirit or meaning of the Amendment."

Boyd v United States, 116 U.S. 616; 6 S.Ct. 524; 29 L. Ed. 746 (1886)

If you think that you have been lied to by your government, you have. But don't be too hard on yourself. After all, who of us were taught this in school? Just be thankful that you're learning it now. Now, let's get back to the three blind mice. The I.R.S. says in Notice 609:

"Our legal right to ask for information is Internal Revenue Code sections 6001, 6011, and 6012(a) and their regulations."

Now read over these three code sections very carefully. Take particular notice of the words that are repeated.

"Section 6001 - Notice or regulations requiring records, statements, and special returns.

Every person liable for any tax imposed by this title, or for the collection thereof, shall keep such records, render such statements, make such returns, and comply with such rules and regulations as the Secretary may from time to time prescribe."

"Section 6011 - General requirement of return, statement, or list.

(a) General rule. When required by regulations prescribed by the Secretary any person made liable for any tax imposed by this title, or with respect to the collection thereof, shall make a return or statement according to the forms and regulations prescribed by the Secretary. Every person required to make a return or statement shall include therein the information required by such forms or regulations."

"Section 6012 - Persons required to make returns of income.

(a) General rule. Returns with respect to income taxes under subtitle A shall be made by the following:

(1)(A) Every individual having for the taxable year gross income which equals or exceeds the exemption amount, except that a return shall not be required of an individual—"

WHO, ME? A NATURAL PERSON?

I love the word "assume." Ever since I was told that the definition of assume is "to make an ass out of you and me" I have been in love with the word. If you have assumed that the words "every person liable" in Section 6001, "any person made liable" in Section 6011, and "every individual" in Section 6012 include you, then you have assumed exactly what the government wants you to—that you are a person made liable to file and pay income taxes. But what you are about to learn will change your mind. The truth is that you are a natural person.

A "natural person," or human being, is recognized in law as a living Soul in human form. This concept is expressed in Genesis 2:7 in the Old Testament where it says, "Then the Lord God formed the man from the dust of the ground and breathed into his nostrils the breath of life, and the man became a living Soul." The King James Version of the Bible translates this passage differently, referring to man as a "living being" rather than a "living Soul." But my personal view is that I am a living Soul in human form. In other words, I do not have a soul; I am a soul.

Regardless of how you define yourself, whether as a living Soul who happens to have a human body or as a human being who just happens to have a Soul, you are acknowledged in law as a "human person" or "natural person." Our Founding Fathers left no confusion in stating the nature of our relationship to God in the Declaration of Independence when they said:

"We hold these truths to be self-evident, that all men are created equal, that they are endowed by their Creator with certain unalienable Rights, that among these are Life, Liberty and the pursuit of Happiness."

Thus, constitutionally, we are acknowledged as aspects of the Creator who, in exercise of our power and authority, created a government. Simply put, the federal United States Government is something that we created. We created it by placing words on a piece of paper, words which have no meaning unless we give them meaning by making a commitment to them. In this way, the government is akin to a piece of paper. It doesn't have life as you and I have life; it has no essence or soul. It has only those limited powers which you and I give it. It is commonly understood that the creation does not rule the creator. As one of the creators of our government, did you ever give your creation the right to tax you directly?

TAXABLE YOU

The government has the right to tax "every person liable," "any person made liable," and "every individual" because all of these are creations of the government. The rule is this: What the government creates it can tax.

Now that you have been given some background into what constitutes a "natural person," let's look at Internal Revenue Code section 7701(a) to see how the I.R.S. defines a "person":

"(1) Person. The term 'person' shall be construed to mean and

include an individual, a trust, estate, partnership, association, company or corporation."

Do you remember from algebra that you cannot mix apples and oranges? You will notice that trusts, estates, partnerships, associations, companies, and corporations are all paper creations. That is to say that they have no soul or essence. In order to be consistent with 7701(a)(1), the "individual" listed must also refer to a paper creation. And, indeed, it does. According to 5 USC 552(a)(2), the term "individual" means either a citizen of the (District) United States or an alien lawfully admitted for permanent residence.

The government thinks of you as a "person" or "individual" because you became one when you obtained a Social Security card. Up until that time, you were a natural person who was outside of the jurisdiction of the federal United States.

What was it about your application for a Social Security card that changed your status from that of a natural person to that of a creation of government? You voluntarily became a U.S. citizen when you checked the little box that said, "Check here if you are a U.S. citizen."

26 CFR 1-1.1(c) defines a U.S. citizen in the following way:

"Every person born or naturalized in the United States and subject to its jurisdiction is a citizen."

Thus, according to Caesar's logic, as the recipient of a valuable right (citizenship) which the government created, you are a citizen of the government. And what the government creates the government can tax.

THE WAY OUT

Luckily, most of us were underage when we got our Social Security card and, therefore, cannot be held legally responsible for what we did. But even if you got your card after becoming of age, you can still rescind your signature on all government contracts by stating under oath that you were mistaken when you said that you were a U.S. citizen.

WE THE PEOPLE ARE SOVEREIGN

How much longer are you going to allow yourself to be treated as a piece of property which is owned, controlled, and used by the government?

We are children of the Supreme Sovereign or God, Creator of the people, and we are endowed with unalienable rights, some of which are stated in the Declaration of Independence, the Constitution, and the Bill of Rights. We the People have absolute sovereign authority over everything that we create. We the People created the Declaration of Independence, the Constitution, and the Bill of Rights. We created the country and the government. We have rights granted to us by our Creator which are over and above the government which we created—rights that cannot be repealed or restrained by any human law, at any time, in any place.

We are sovereigns, the highest ranking power and authority. As sovereigns, we established the Constitution, the country, and the government. This thing that we call the federal United States Government is an abomination and a perversion—an ugly cancer that has infested our lives and perverted our consciousness. This must be changed, and it must be changed now. It will require that we work together in harmony, with a clear purpose, to re-establish our Constitution as the supreme law of the land. The need is clear, the objective is in sight, and the call to action has been sounded.

Three Blind Mice, Three Blind Mice,
See how they run, See how they run,
They all ran after the farmer's wife,
She cut off their tails with a carving knife,
Have you ever seen such a sight
in your life, as Three Blind Mice?

CAUGHT IN THE TRAP

For the year Jan. 1–Dec. 31, 1994, or other tax year beginning _____ 1994, ending ____, 19

Your social security number

Spouse's social security no.

Use the IRS label. Otherwise, please print or type.

Note: Checking "Yes" will not change your tax or reduce your refund.

Presidential Election Campaign ▶ Do you want $3 to go to this fund? ....
If a joint return, does your spouse want $3 to go to this fund?

For Privacy Act and Paperwork Reduction Act Notice, see page 4.

Filing Status
(See page 12.)
Check only one box.

1 ☐ Single
2 ☐ Married filing joint return (even if only one had income)
3 ☐ Married filing separate return. Enter spouse's SSN above full name here ▶
4 ☐ Head of household (with qualifying person). (See page 13.) If qualifying person is a child but not your dependent, enter this child's name here. ▶
5 ☐ Qualifying widow(er) with dependent child (yr. spouse died ▶19 0) (See page 13.)

Exemptions
(See page 13.)

6a ☐ Yourself. If your parent (or someone else) can claim you as a dependent on his/her tax return, do not check box 6a. But be sure to check box on line 33b on page 2

No. of boxes checked on 6a and 6b ▶ 0

b ☐ Spouse ....

c Dependents:

(1) Name (first, initial, and last name)	(2) Chk. if under age 1	(3) If age 1 or older, dependent's social security number	(4) Dependent's relationship to you	(5) No. of mos. lived in your home in 1994

If more than six dependents, see page 14.

No. of your children on 6c who
• lived with you   0
• didn't live with you due to divorce or separation (see page 14)   0

Dependents on 6c not entered above   0

d If your child didn't live with you but is claimed as your dependent under a pre-1985 agreement, check here ▶ ☐

e Total number of exemptions claimed ....

Add numbers entered on lines above ▶ 0

Income

Attach Copy B of your Forms W-2, W-2G, and 1099-R here.

If you did not get a W-2, see page 15.

Enclose, but do not attach, any payment with your return.

7 Wages, salaries, tips, etc. Attach Form(s) W-2 .... | 7 | 0
8a Taxable interest income (see page 15). Attach Schedule B if over $400 .... | 8a | 0
b Tax-exempt interest (see page 15). DON'T include on line 8a | 8b | 0
9 Dividend income. Attach Schedule B if over $400 .... | 9 | 0
10 Taxable refunds, credits, or offsets of state and local income taxes (see page 16) | 10 | 0
11 Alimony received .... | 11 | 0
12 Business income or (loss). Attach Schedule C or C-EZ .... | 12 | 0
13 Capital gain or (loss). If required, attach Schedule D (see page 16) .... | 13 | 0
14 Other gains or (losses). Attach Form 4797 .... | 14 | 0
15a Total IRA distributions .. | 15a | 0 | b Taxable amount (see pg. 17) | 15b | 0
16a Total pensions and annuities | 16a | 0 | b Taxable amount (see pg. 17) | 16b | 0
17 Rental real estate, royalties, partnerships, S corporations, trusts, etc. Attach Schedule E .... | 17 | 0
18 Farm income or (loss). Attach Schedule F .... | 18 | 0
19 Unemployment compensation (see page 18) .... | 19 | 0
20a Social security benefits | 20a | 0 | b Taxable amount (see pg. 18) | 20b | 0
21 Other income. .... | 21 | 0
22 Add the amounts in the far right column for lines 7 through 21. This is your total income ▶ | 22 | 0

Adjustments to Income

Caution: See instructions ▶

23a Your IRA deduction (see page 19) .... | 23a | 0
b Spouse's IRA deduction (see page 19) | 23b | 0
24 Moving expenses. Attach Form 3903 or 3903-F .... | 24 | 0
25 One-half of self-employment tax .... | 25 | 0
26 Self-employed health insurance deduction (see page 21) .. | 26 | 0
27 Keogh retirement plan, self-employed SEP deduction ... | 27 | 0
28 Penalty on early withdrawal of savings .... | 28 | 0
29 Alimony paid. Recipient's SSN ▶ | 29 | 0
30 Add lines 23a through 29. These are your total adjustments .... 0 ▶ | 30 | 0

Adj. Gr. Income

31 Subtract line 30 from line 22. This is your adjusted gross income .... ▶ | 31 | 0

3402   Form 1040 (1994)

ARE YOU A TAXPAYER?

You are if you fit the I.R.S.'s definition of a taxpayer.

"Section 1313. Definitions.

b) Taxpayer. Notwithstanding section 7701(a)(14), the term 'taxpayer' means any person subject to a tax under the applicable revenue law."

"Section 7701. Definitions.

(a) When used in this title, where not otherwise distinctly expressed or manifestly incompatible with the intent thereof—

(1) Person. The term 'person' shall be construed to mean and include an individual, a trust, estate, partnership, association, company or corporation.

(14) Taxpayer. The term 'taxpayer' means any person subject to any internal revenue tax."

From the point of view of the I.R.S., a "taxpayer" is a person. But a "person" is defined as an "individual." We, therefore, can conclude that trusts, estates, partnerships, associations, companies, and corporations are the individual persons required to file 1040 U.S. Individual Income Tax Returns.

Do you remember the old saying, "If the shoe fits, wear it"? Well, if you fit the I.R.S.'s definition of taxpayer, then pay the tax.

From what you have been learning, you obviously know that you are not a person or individual in the same classification as the aforementioned paper creations of government. But you have made yourself a taxpayer by entering into certain agreements. Among those agreements are the Social Security number you possess and the W-4 you signed when you were hired for your job.

No Law?
What Do You Mean, No Law?

Just as there is no law that requires you to file an income tax return unless you are a person made liable, there is also no law that requires you to have or give a Social Security number in order to get a job. In fact, the law says just the opposite. Actually, it is unlawful for any employer to discriminate against you because you refuse to give a Social Security number or sign a W-4. Unfortunately, there is a big gap between what the law says and what some think that the law says.

When you were hired for your last job, your employer probably handed you a stack of papers. Among those papers was a W-4. When you filled out the W-4, you voluntarily classified yourself as a "taxpayer."

It is understandable that your employer did not know the law any better than you did. Your employer probably neither knew the difference between a direct tax and an indirect tax nor that there is even a classification called "non-taxpayer!"

"The revenue laws are a code or system in regulation of tax assessment and collection. They relate to taxpayers, and not to nontaxpayers. The latter are without their scope. No procedure is prescribed for nontaxpayers, and no attempt is made to annul any of their rights and remedies in due course of law. With them Congress does not assume to deal, and they are neither of the subject nor of the object of the revenue laws."

Long v Rasmussen, 281 F 236, 238 (1922)

Again and again you can find Supreme Court decisions that point the way out of the voluntary tax system. See Economy Plumbing and Heating v U.S., 470 F2d 585 (1792).

Unless you have made yourself liable by engaging in a taxable activity, such as selling drugs, practicing law, issuing bank notes, or doing business in a corporate capacity (which is not a natural right), you are not the subject of the income tax laws. If you are not the subject or the object of the income tax laws, then you should know the following:

- ☛ There is no law that requires you to obtain a Social Security number.
- ☛ There is no law that requires you to provide a Social Security number as a condition for getting a job.

☞ There is no law that requires you to sign a W-4.

☞ There is no law that requires your employer to turn over to the federal government any W-4 that you may have signed.

☞ There is no law that can force you to waive any of your constitutional rights.

Therefore, you cannot be forced to give testimony against yourself. When you sign a 1040 U.S. Individual Income Tax Return under penalty of perjury, you are voluntarily giving up your rights, and anything you place on that form can be used against you in a court of law.

All of the above and a great deal more you have done, and are doing, voluntarily. You have ensnared yourself in the trap of paying income taxes.

Our Constitution makes it perfectly clear that no government has the power or authority to tax a God-given right. Your right to lawfully acquire property or compensation by contracting your own labor in an innocent, harmless, and lawful manner cannot be taxed. So tell me, why are you still paying taxes?

I'M A TAXPAYER

I pay all of the lawful taxes that I am required to pay. Every item that I purchase is taxed to some extent. I don't remember the exact number, or even if this is true, but someone once told me that there were over 100 taxes on a loaf of bread. Regardless of the actual number, we all pay taxes when we buy a loaf of bread. But, when I found out that there was no law requiring me to pay federal, state, or Social Security taxes, I said, "Thank you," and exited the system legally.

As soon as I got free from the system, I began telling everyone I could the good news. I was amazed at some of the reactions. A few, like you, wanted to know more. They were motivated enough to want to get themselves out of the system. But most were locked in fear. They had read too many I.R.S. horror stories. Many had faced the I.R.S. in the past and lost—big time. There were so many stories, so many reasons, and they all came down to fear—fear which has been carefully cultivated, by the I.R.S. in order to keep you in line.

What you fear the most you will, inevitably, have to face. In fact, the longer you put off dealing with fear, the more formidable it becomes until, finally, something happens that forces you to come face to face with it. When that happens, you wonder why it took you so long. Fear of the I.R.S. is no different than any other fear. The time is quickly coming when you will be forced to deal with it.

If yours is a two-income family, pause for a moment, and consider this: If both of you are working to make ends meet, what would be the effect on the family if one of you no longer paid federal, state, or Social Security taxes? Could the family live better? For most families, the answer is yes. One person working full-time, with no deductions, earns a household income that is equal to or greater than two people working and paying taxes. If this is your situation, then, the longer you hesitate, the more it is costing you.

It is costing you in terms of your pocketbook. It is costing you in terms of your health. It is costing you in terms of the amount of time you spend with your family and loved ones. And it is costing you in terms of your personal freedom. For every day that you could be joining the chorus of awakening Souls who are standing up for themselves and don't, it is costing you. We, who have already conquered our fear, ask you to join us.

THE NEXT STEP

Want more money in your paycheck? Me, too. That's why I voluntarily withdrew from the income tax system four years ago. What I have done you can also do. You can do it on your own, or you can hire me and my staff as your guides. Either way, here is what you need to do first: Call the I.R.S. at 1-800-829-1040 and ask them this question: "What law or statute makes me liable to file an individual income tax return?" This one question holds the key to your success, and the reason is this: If you cannot force yourself to make the call, then you will never take the steps necessary to get out of the system. It's as simple as that.

No matter what the I.R.S. tells you, write it down. Don't take my or anyone else's word for it. Call and find out the answer for yourself. The I.R.S. might tell you that the Sixteenth Amendment is the law that gives them the authority to tax you. But the Sixteenth Amendment gives Congress the authority to tax "income." What you earn for your labor is "wages." More than likely, the I.R.S. will cite a section of the Internal Revenue Code, also known as Title 26. But a quick phone call or trip to the library will reveal that the Internal Revenue Code is not law—that it has never been enacted into positive law and is merely prima facie law, which is only presumed to be true until disproven by evidence to the contrary.

After completing your research and discovering on your own that there is no law which makes you liable to file an individual income tax return, take action. At the very least, call and order the video "Liberty in the Balance." This is the video that I recommend to anyone interested in getting out of the system. If you enjoy reading, I highly recommend the book, "I.R.S. Humbug." Each of these is available from me, postage-paid, for $24.95 and $29.95, respectively. If you are interested in purchasing our Educational Package, for $59.95 we'll send you the video and book just mentioned, plus a copy of the Constitution, a booklet on the subject of Common Law Unincorporated Trusts, 1 issue of *Anti-Shyster* magazine, 1 issue of *Connecting Link* magazine, and a list of answers to the questions most commonly asked about The De-Taxing America Program.

If you were to spend 80-100 hours studying, you would probably be able to write and file the documents necessary to legally remove yourself from the income tax system. But, if you don't have the time to do all of the work yourself, you have the option of hiring me and my staff to do the work for you. Our fee for The De-Taxing America Program is $795 for individuals and $995 for couples. The fee may be paid all at once or with 50% down and two payments of 25% each.

For your money, my staff and I will prepare 2 volumes of legal reference materials for you, including 28 personalized letters for you to file with various agencies and departments of federal and state government in three separate mailings over a two to three-month period. Some of the documents that you will be sending require a response. When you receive these responses, send them to us and we will answer them for you.

We also do common law, unincorporated trusts to help our clients to protect their assets and maintain their privacy. The charge for the first trust is $495. Each additional trust is $150.

Start now by calling me, Barrie Konicov, at (616) 891-2217. I'll have you request a new Form W-4 from your employer, read it over, and, this time, using what you know to be true, fill it out properly by marking it "exempt." You may need to fill out a separate form for Social Security taxes, but, within a week or so, your employer should stop withholding federal, state, and Social Security taxes from your wages.

THE GREAT
SNOW JOB

PART II

THE STORY
OF MONEY

THE STORY OF MONEY

Reflect with me for a moment upon the nature of money, wealth, and prosperity. The more time you take reflecting upon it, the more varied and abstract your thoughts concerning money, wealth and prosperity will become.

"Consider, first, money, and soon your mind will guide you to understand the true nature of money. And you will know that the value of money is determined by you, with every transaction that you enter. You will know that the value of money is determined by the number of zeros on the bill. And a zero is nothing."

I wrote those words several years ago as an introduction to a tape entitled "Money and Prosperity." The tape was and is marketed under the Potentials Unlimited label. What we call money is not money, and the only value it has is the value that you and I give it. The pieces of paper you and I pass around are Federal Reserve Notes. They look like money to us because we have been told that they are money and because they spend like money, but they are not money. They are an instrument that is being used to enslave us. Unless we collectively wake up to the reality of our money system and our government, we are in for a huge upheaval.

Money is meant to be a medium of exchanging value for value. But the creation of money is in the hands of individuals who are controlling us by the use of debt. There is a way out of the debt system for all souls willing to take control of their lives and to stand up for themselves.

To understand the problem, let me explain how paper began to circulate as money:

Imagine that you are in England around 1660, at a time when the only money around is gold and silver coins. These are minted and put into circulation by the king. When the king is short of gold or silver and in need of something, he adulterates the money by diluting the gold with copper. The newly-minted coins are the same size but with less gold. It doesn't matter if his subjects refuse to accept these adulterated coins. The king merely has his court rule that the money is worth whatever he says it is worth. After all, he is the king.

Imagine that you have worked hard and saved some money. Where will you put that money for safekeeping? In most communities, there is a goldsmith who has a large iron box where he keeps gold and silver. You ask the goldsmith to keep your gold and silver in his safe. He agrees, and you pay him a fee for his service. As proof that he has your gold and silver, he issues you a receipt.

The next time you want to buy something, rather than redeeming your certificate and using the gold to buy whatever you want, you use your gold receipt. It's quicker and easier. As long as the seller can go to the goldsmith and redeem the certificate for gold, everything works out fine. This is probably how paper receipts began to circulate as money.

Now, place yourself in the position of the goldsmith. How long would it take you to figure out that very few people ever come at the same time to redeem their gold certificates? One day, like the king, you find yourself short of gold and silver. Could you say no to temptation? Or would you tell yourself, "I'll just issue a gold receipt without any gold to back it up because, after all, no one is going to check on me, and I'll have the gold in a few days?"

You quickly learn that spending your own gold receipts causes certain unsettling questions to be asked. You come up with a new plan that gives you something for nothing but doesn't make it too noticeable. Your plan is simple: You loan gold receipts and collect interest. As long as you don't get too greedy, you can get away with this something-for-nothing scheme. Soon you and other goldsmiths/bankers are lending four times as many paper receipts as you have in gold.

This process got a boost when the King of England was in need of a great deal of money to fight a war. The king turned to William Paterson.

Paterson and his friends pooled their resources and came up with £72,000 in gold and silver. But, instead of lending the gold and silver directly to the king, they formed a bank and printed paper receipts equal to 16$2/3$ times the value of their gold and silver reserves. They lent the king £1.2 million at 8$1/3$% interest per year. The yearly interest was £100,000. The king didn't care; he had a war to fight. After all, he would simply raise the taxes on his subjects to pay the interest. (Sound familiar?)

Paterson and his friends were protected. They had the foresight to lend their paper receipts to the government. Since these receipts were needed to fight a war, the king couldn't allow them to fail. He declared them legal tender. These receipts were now regarded as being the same as the gold for which they had stood. A new golden rule came into being; THEM THAT HAVE THE GOLD ... RULE!

Since paper money first began circulating, the situation has changed little. When the federal government wants more money, it borrows it from and through the private banking system, the Federal Reserve. The owners of the Federal Reserve are in no need of gold or silver to back up their loans to the government. Their money is legal tender. Unlike Paterson's time, there is no gold or silver in the system. The bankers are still receiving something for nothing. And you, as a subject, give the bankers one-third of your time when you pay federal, state, and Social Security taxes.

Most everyone knows that, at one time, our government actually had gold and silver backing our currency. Some people believe that the gold and silver may still be there. Most people are completely unaware that a few, very rich individuals are in control of this country through their ownership of the privately-owned and operated for profit Federal Reserve Banks.

To understand what is happening with our money today, we need to refer to Article I, Section 8 of the U.S. Constitution, which says: "The Congress shall have Power ... to coin Money, regulate the Value thereof, and of foreign Coin, and fix the Standard of Weights and Measures." It is important to understand that the "power to coin money" does not include the power to print money because, if you have the power to print money, then you end up with paper money that is worthless—just as worthless as the receipts issued by the dishonest goldsmith.

To ensure that no one but Congress had control of this country's money, the Founding Fathers also added Article I, Section 10, which reads: "No State shall...coin Money; emit Bills of Credit; make any Thing but gold and silver Coin a Tender in Payment of Debts ..." With these two articles of our Constitution in place, the Founding Fathers felt that they had ensured the stability of the country's money supply.

In 1792, Congress passed the first Coinage Act, which set the Standard Unit of Value and the ratio of gold to silver. A dollar of gold was defined as 24 8/10 grains pure 9/10 fine, and a coin dollar of silver was defined as 371.25 grains .999 fine or 412.5 grains Standard Silver.

Several times in our country's history Congress has enacted laws which have violated the constitutional provision governing money. The last time Congress unlawfully turned over its responsibility to manage the country's money supply was with the enactment of the Federal Reserve Act in 1913. For a period of time, the Federal Reserve willingly exchanged gold and silver for paper certificates on demand. But, as the depression of 1929 deepened, Congress passed a law making it unlawful to own gold, and, in 1933, the banks stopped redeeming paper money with gold. By 1968, all that was left supporting our money was silver, and then that was removed by presidential order.

Today, there is no gold or silver backing up our currency—only the full faith and credit of the United States Government. The federal government has pledged you and your ability to earn money as collateral to the international bankers for over $4 trillion in loans. This is a great deal for the bankers. The bankers put up nothing, and you, as a slave, turn over to the bankers one-third of your income to pay your "fair share" of the federal income tax. Your income tax does not pay for the running of the federal government. It pays the interest on the national debt—a debt that was created as a bookkeeping entry.

The federal government is out of control. In 1992, it spent $1,448 trillion. That's $3,967,123,000 each day of the year. The cost to the average household was $291 a week, an increase of $41 a week over the 1991 budget. Now every dollar that the federal government collects in individual income taxes goes to pay the interest on the national debt.

In my opinion, there cannot be a single member of Congress who is not aware of what is going on. They know that this country is heading for financial ruin because they have consciously acted to bring that about. There is very little that you and I can do to stop this from happening. There is one thing, however, that you can do to protect yourself and your family. Stop paying the slave masters. Stop paying income taxes, and place the money you save into gold and silver because you are going to need it soon.

LOCAL BANK FRAUD

The fraud of the bankers does not stop with the owners of the Federal Reserve. It continues through our system and includes every bank, every savings and loan, and every credit card company. The fraud reaches into every banking transaction that you have ever been a party to.

Consider this scenario. You want to buy a used car. You arrange for a loan from your bank (bank A) and fill out the papers. The banker gives you a check made payable to the car dealer for $5,000. You give the check to the car dealer. The dealer turns the car over to you and deposits the $5,000 check into his bank (bank B). It happens all the time.

Now, let's take a deeper look at the transaction. Did any money leave the bank? No. The money never left the bank because the banker didn't give you any. He gave you *bank credit*. The courts have ruled that "A check is not money." See School Dist., 47 Joint, Columbia County v U.S. National Bank of Portland, 187 Ore 360; 211 P. 2d 723 (1949). They have also ruled that "A check is an order on a bank to pay money." See Young et al v Hembree, 181 OKL 202; 73 P. 2d 393 (1937). The courts have further ruled that "National banks may lend their money but not their credit." See Norton Grocery Co. v People's National Bank of Abingdon, 151 Va 195; 144 S.E. 501 (1928). The courts have made such rulings because, unlike the Federal Reserve Banks, local banks are not allowed by law to create money. However, they do it all the time.

WHAT IS BANK CREDIT?

Bank credit is the biggest fraud going. It is the creation of bills of credit by private corporations for their private gain. This is one of the most important issues we have to face today because 95% of the nation's money supply consists of bank credit.

Bank credit, unlike Federal Reserve Notes, is not something tangible that you can see or hold. The closest you will ever get to seeing bank credit is to look at your checkbook or credit card. Essentially, bank credit is nothing more than the creation of numbers which are added to your checking account in a bank's bookkeeping department. When you write a check, numbers which represent dollars are transferred from your checking account to someone else's checking account. The creation, transfer, and use of bookkeeping entries as money is what bank credit is all about.

Bank credit is first created when you take out a loan and the banker hands you a check. This check is not money, but rather a promise from the bank to pay you money. The bank might have enough money to cash your check, assuming that everyone doesn't bring his or her checks in at the same time.

The basis for the fraud charge is that the bank has written a check against funds which do not exist. The banker gambles that you will use your checking account in place of cash. Most of the time, the banker is right. People usually deposit the checks that they receive into their checking accounts and then spend them by writing other checks against the bookkeeping entries which have been added to their account.

Most people do not know that a check is not money, that bank credit is not lawful money, and that the courts have consistently ruled against the banks for lending credit.

FRACTIONAL BANKING

When the car dealer deposits your check into his account, bank

B then has access to 5,000 more dollars that it can make loans against. Modern banking regulations allow banks to loan up to 90% of all money deposited. With sleight of hand and the blessing of modern bookkeeping entries, bank B can now lend an additional $4,500 (90% of $5,000). A different customer at bank B wants a loan. He or she borrows the $4,500 and deposits it in bank C. Now bank C can loan 90% of the $4,500 ($4,050). All of the banks (A, B, and C) charge interest on each of the loans.[1] The process can go on indefinitely. This bank credit was created out of thin air. Now you understand more clearly what I meant by "....the value of money is determined by the number of zeros on the bill. And a zero is nothing."

Most of us have several of these bank loans. Many of you have been forced into bankruptcy and forced to give up your homes because of this fraudulent system.

STAND UP

I urge you to stand up for yourself. You are your own sovereign being, not a piece of property to be owned, controlled, or used as collateral for bank loans. The federal government is controlled by the owners of the Federal Reserve Bank. Through their control of the nation's monetary system, the bankers use your labor and property as collateral to give value to their printing press money (Federal Reserve Notes) and bank credit.

Under their system, each dollar placed into circulation is borrowed. Their system works by expanding debt. Only borrowing creates the interest needed to pay off existing loans. You could call this debt-and-slave-money system the "missing dollar."

Imagine that there are only $10 in existence. I lend them to you under the condition that you give me some collateral and repay me $11. If you agree to this, then you have agreed to the impossible. It is impossible to repay me $11 because the additional $1 does not exist. All I lent you was $10, and that is all of the money in existence. When the debt is due, you will either have to borrow the $1 in interest or lose the collateral.

The federal government debt is massive, as is the debt of the business and private sectors of the economy. The debt will continue to grow because this is how our slave masters have designed the system. As a slave, your time is controlled by interest payments and taxes that take three and one-half days of your labor out of five. Is it any wonder that you cannot get ahead? Is it any wonder that you are unable to provide a reasonable level of comfort for you and your family?

Our Founding Fathers bequeathed to us a system which was free from the enslavement of the money lenders. We the People have allowed the money lenders, operating through the government, to enslave us once again. It is time to return this country to its original Constitutional form of government. It is time for We the People to stand up and say no.

Stand up and say no to a fraudulent money and tax system that steals your labor. Stand up to a government that has pledged you and your assets as collateral to a small group of bankers who are drunk with power and intoxicated by their own sense of self-importance.

Stand up and let the words of Abraham Lincoln vibrate anew through this land, *"that this nation, under God, will have a new birth of freedom, that government of the people, by the people, and for the people shall not perish from this land."* Stand up, and your courage will inspire others to do the same.

---

[1] The Federal Reserve Bank of New York offers *The Story of Banks*, an illustrated booklet that explores the creation of money, credit, bank loans, and more. For free copies, call (212) 720-6134.

* Some of the information in this chapter came from the book, *The Paper Aristocracy*, by Howard S. Katz. 1976. Out of print.

The Story of Fraud and Slavery

When I was in high school, my parents became partners in a drug store in downtown Louisville, Kentucky. To earn spending money, I worked evenings and weekends during school and full-time during the summer. The drug store offered a full line of products and services. There was one service that really caught my attention: check-printing. Most of the people that the store served did not have their own checking accounts, so they relied on the drug store's checks to pay their monthly bills. I can remember being fascinated by that check-writing machine. When there was a lull in business, I would slip a piece of paper into the machine, adjust the keys, and write out a check for any amount my imagination dictated. I often dreamed of having such a magic machine, one that could simply create money—endless amounts of money.

Who wouldn't want a magic money machine? After reading "The Story of Money," you probably know that such a machine exists and that it is in the hands of an elite group of people called bankers. All bankers have to do to create money is to slip a piece of paper into a magic money machine, push a few buttons, and out comes money. Follow along with me, now, while I take you down the yellow brick road of fraud and slavery.

Secured Credit Cards

Suppose for a moment that you have bad or limited credit and that you apply for a credit card. Given these circumstances, you would be required to put up some collateral. The bank would probably ask you to open a certificate of deposit (CD) for 125% of the credit card's credit limit. (If the credit card had a limit of $1,000, you would have to put up $1,250 in collateral.)

Note that the bank has nothing at risk when you use your credit card. You have made arrangements with the bank to lend you up to $1,000. You have promised to pay them according to the terms and conditions of the note you signed. The question is: Where does the bank get the money you're borrowing? Some people think that it comes from the money in your CD, but that is not the case. The truth is that the PROMISSORY NOTE which you signed is now an asset of the bank's and, based upon this PROMISE to pay, the bank created bank credit, which it lent to you.

The bank doesn't reduce the amount of your CD as you make purchases or take out loans. As the bills come into the bank, it pays the merchant for your purchases by electronically transferring numbers in its computer. If, for any reason, you do not pay for your purchases, then the bank has the authority to use the money in your CD to cover your credit card debt.

A MORTGAGE NOTE

Suppose that you go to your bank to borrow money for a home. You fill out the application, and the bank runs a check on you. You pass with flying colors, and, next, you sign all of the papers. Of course, you will have to make a deposit on your home, just like you did with the credit card. The bank will have you sign a PROMISSORY NOTE, or mortgage, just as you did with the credit card. The bank takes the title to your home as collateral, as it did with the CD. And, if you default on your payments, then the bank will foreclose on your home and sell it, just as they would use your CD to cover your credit card debt.

The same question arises: Where did the bank get the money it lent you for your home? Answer: It didn't lend you any money. It lent you its credit. Based on the asset of your signature on the PROMISSORY NOTE, the bank issued a check from the magic money machine which was accepted as money.

You know that a check is not money from "The Story of Money." It is a PROMISE to pay money. Bingo. The bank lied to you. You thought that you were borrowing money, but the bank lent you credit. In good faith, you entered into what you thought was an honest transaction. But the fact that the transaction was suspect was known only to the bank (and to the courts which have ruled that it is illegal for a bank to lend its credit). In legal terms, you have been defrauded because *your* PROMISE to pay was backed by collateral (the title to your home), while *their* PROMISE to pay was backed by nothing (neither gold nor silver). In effect, the bank, which risked nothing by lending you the credit that it created, now has your deposit, your PROMISE to pay, and the title to your home.

STATE BORROWING

When your state is short of money, it also borrows from the banks. A state's PROMISE to pay is called a bond. These PROMISES to pay are based upon the state's ability to get you to pay. The bank accepts the bonds as an asset and does the same sleight of hand with the state that it did with you. It gives the state a check from the magic money machine. The state deposits the check back into the bank and writes more checks on the check. Again, ask yourself this: Did the bank lend your state any money in return for its PROMISE to pay? No! Once again, the bank wrote a check, which is not money.

Much of the money that your state collects from you in taxes goes toward paying the principal and interest on these fraudulent bank loans. You and I and our ability to pay, along with our property, homes, cars, etc., are pledged as collateral to the bankers for these loans. The bankers put up little of value. They use their magic money machine, and you pay and pay and pay.

THE FEDERAL GOVERNMENT AND THE NATIONAL DEBT

It's the same story. The federal government issues a bond. The bond goes to the privately-owned Federal Reserve Bank. The bond is a PROMISE to pay based upon the government's ability to collect taxes from you and me. Again, the bankers issue a check from the magic money machine. And, again, you pay and pay and pay. As I said before, the vast majority, if not all, of our country's income tax revenues go to pay the interest on the national debt—a debt that was created by the magic money machine.

WHAT ... IS THIS MONEY?

The Constitution says that money is gold or silver, probably because gold and silver are rare metals which require someone's labor to put them in a form which we can use. This has never been changed. The Constitution also says that only Congress has the authority to coin or regulate the value of money. We got into this mess because Congress committed treason to the Constitution by illegally turning over to a group of bankers its responsibility to coin and regulate the value of money.

The way out of this mess is for We the People to reinstate the Constitution as the Supreme Law of the Land. Until and unless we do so, this fraudulent money, banking, and taxing system will continue to enslave us.

BUT IT WORKS!

I know that there will be those of you who say, "Yes, Barrie, I know that, based upon your information, the system is dishonest. But it works, and that's what matters to me." My answer to you is this: You can remain a slave or you can free yourself, but no one can free you but yourself. Keep these two points in mind: First, usury, which is having to pay back both the principal and the interest on a loan, is in violation of Biblical law, which demands "just weights and measures." Second, there is always a price to be paid for dishonesty. For most of the history of this country, we operated under an honest, constitutional system. And, if we allow the dishonesty to continue our sense of freedom could dull to the point where not one of us is able to recognize the fact that we are enslaved.

VOLUNTARY SLAVERY

What do you call a person whose time is controlled by another person? I call that person a slave. The Thirteenth Amendment to the Constitution abolished involuntary servitude. But it does allow voluntary slavery. If you choose to give up two to three and a half days of your labor each week to voluntary taxation and fraudulent interest, then you may. But if you feel a calling deep inside of you, a small voice whispering words of personal power and responsibility, a voice that is building, demanding that you stand up and free yourself, then follow that voice. Stand up, lift your head high, and look around. You will find that others are standing tall and proud with you.

SIGN THIS PLEDGE

I, _____, pledge my support to the Constitution of the United States of America and to the Republic which it created, one people, under God, with equal liberty and justice for all.

It is a given that not everyone knows the story of *The Great Snow Job*. But, now that you do, you must do something.

DON'T FEED THE HAND THAT BITES YOU

For the past 25 years I have known that the owners of the Federal Reserve Bank control the country. But, until recently, I did not understand the extent of the fraud in the banking system. I began my research in preparation for writing *The Great Snow Job* by talking to several judges and attorneys about the money and banking system.

I discovered that most of them do not know the truth about our money and banking system. I investigated further and found that schools, on all levels, do not teach that banks create money out of thin air. I looked through history books, accounting books, and law books on both the high school and college level, and the truth is not there. I talked to teachers, lawyers, and bankers, and no one I talked to knew that banks create money out of thin air. Or, at least, if they did know, they weren't talking.

But I did find the truth verified in an unlikely source and in a form that cannot be contradicted—The Federal Reserve Bank of Chicago's own publication, "Modern Money Mechanics." The booklet is free, and you can get several copies for your family and friends by calling 1-312-322-5111. The following is an excerpt from that publication.

READ SLOWLY AND SAVOR

"Money is such a routine part of everyday living that its existence and acceptance ordinarily are taken for granted. A user may sense that money must come into being either automatically as a result of economic activity or as an outgrowth of some government operation. But just how this happens all too often remains a mystery.

"The actual process of money creation takes place primarily in banks ... In the absence of legal reserve requirements, banks

can build up deposits by increasing loans and investments so long as they keep enough currency on hand to redeem whatever amounts the holders of deposits want to convert into currency. This unique attribute of the banking business was discovered many centuries ago.

"It started with goldsmiths. As early bankers, they initially provided safekeeping services, making a profit from vault storage fees for gold and coins deposited with them. People would redeem their 'deposit receipts' whenever they needed gold or coins to purchase something, and physically take the gold or coins to the seller who, in turn, would deposit them for safekeeping, often with the same banker. Everyone soon found that it was a lot easier simply to use the deposit receipts directly as a means of payment. These receipts, which became known as notes, were acceptable as money since whoever held them could go to the banker and exchange them for metallic money.

"Then, bankers discovered that they could make loans merely by giving their promises to pay, or bank notes, to borrowers. In this way, banks began to create money. More notes could be issued than the gold and coin on hand because only a portion of the notes outstanding would be presented for payment at any one time. Enough metallic money had to be kept on hand, of course, to redeem whatever volume of notes was presented for payment.

"Transaction deposits are the modern counterpart of bank notes. It was a small step from printing notes to making book entries crediting deposits of borrowers, which the borrowers in turn could 'spend' by writing checks, thereby 'printing' their own money."

Modern Money Mechanics—A Workbook on Bank Reserves and Deposits Expansion, Pages 2 and 3, Feb. 1994, Federal Reserve Bank of Chicago.

Reading *Modern Money Mechanics* absolutely delighted me! Whoever authorized this booklet to be written, published, and placed into distribution is owed a great debt of gratitude. This booklet, read, understood, and acted upon by you, will evolve the system as you do your part to free We the People.

TO CATCH A THIEF

Let's apply what you have been learning about money and banking to buying a home. Let us suppose that, after years of saving and months of looking, you finally find a home that you love. You know that interest rates vary from bank to bank so you shop around until you find the best deal. You are somewhat nervous as you sit down with a loan officer. But, since you have built your credit over the years, there should be no problem getting the loan. In a week, the bank calls with the good news. Your loan has been approved.

The hard part is over. In a few weeks, you go to the closing, and you are greeted with a mountain of papers. After 25 minutes, you have finished the paper work, and the home is yours and the bank's.

You borrowed $85,000 at 8.5% interest, agreeing to pay it back at $653 per month for the next 30 years. In the next 30 years (assuming that you earn $10 per hour), 23,500 hours of your labor will go toward paying for that house. This works out to about 11-3/4 years at 40 hours per week. This is the system, and that is how it works.

But what you did not know is that the bank just defrauded you. Here is how they did it. As a typical bank customer, you assumed that the money you borrowed from the bank came from its depositors or investors. That is what the bank wants you to believe. But that is not what happened.

Before you borrowed the money from the bank, it did not exist. The bank took your loan application and renamed it a "promissory note." It then took your "promissory note" and attached it to the title of the property. Using the home as collateral, the bank wrote a check.

The moment the bank wrote the check, it created the money. If you doubt that the bank is writing checks to create money, just read the following again. In the Federal Reserve's own words:

"Then, bankers discovered that they could make loans merely by giving their promises to pay, or bank notes, to borrowers. In

this way, banks began to create money."

Now, let's get back to our example. The bank made the check payable to the seller. The seller accepted the check and deposited it back into the system.

You probably think that the bank approved your loan because they believed that you would make good on your promise to pay. Actually, it doesn't really matter to the bank whether you keep your promise or not. After all, if you don't, they will just foreclose and take your home.

What took the bank eight hours to create will take you 23,500 hours of labor to pay back.

Your head should be telling you that there is something wrong with this picture. Let's modify this scenario for a moment and, using the same numbers, make the transaction honest.

Let's say that you bought the same home, on a land contract, directly from the seller. Now you would pay the seller directly. Would the exchange of the home for money be honest? Would it be legal? Yes, it most certainly would be. Why? Because the home is the product of many people's labor. And the money you exchanged for the home has value because you exchanged your labor for it. Unlike the first example with the bank, it was not something which you created out of thin air.

When you exchange your labor for money, the money has value or substance because you exchanged your labor for it. It is your labor which gives value to the money. In this example, value for value is exchanged.

Financing a home through a bank could be an honest transaction. But the bank would have to loan you money which was either invested by its owners or placed on deposit by its customers. Most of us assume when we borrow from a bank that this is where the money comes from. This is what the bankers want us to believe.

THE BUYER/THE CONTRACT/ THE SNOW JOB

As the buyer in our example, you have entered into a contract with the bank. Every contract must have six elements in order to be legally binding. If any one of the elements is missing, then there is no contract. Here are the elements of a contract:

1. Offer by person qualified to make the contract.
   This element is present in the contract in our example.

2. Acceptance by party qualified to make and accept the contract.
   This element is present in the contract in our example.

3. Agreement, full disclosure, and complete understanding by both parties.

Now, let me ask you this. Did you know the last time that you took out a bank loan or used a credit card that the bank was going to create the money out of thin air? If you didn't, then there is no "full disclosure and complete understanding." Therefore, there is no contract.

4. Consideration given.
   When you borrow from a bank which creates money out of thin air, there is no consideration. No consideration, NO CONTRACT.

5. Every contract must have the element of time to make it lawful.
   This element is present in the contract in our example.

6. All parties must be of lawful age, usually 21 years old.
   This element is present in the contract in our example.

79

SUE THE BASTARDS

You have been lied to, cheated, and stolen from every time you have borrowed money from a bank. If you want to help restore this country to a constitutional money system, then here is something practical that you can do. You can sue every bank that has stolen from you and force them to cancel your loans.

It is simpler than you may think to sue. De-Taxing America has already prepared an educational package that you or your attorney can use to sue every bank that has defrauded you. Just think about it for a moment. You could bring an action forcing each of your banks to cancel your debts. If enough of us put pressure on the banks, we could evolve the system sooner than you think.

LIGHTS, CAMERA, ACTION!

The time for action is NOW. Each of you reading this book is somewhat aware of the probable collapse of our economic system. Perhaps you don't believe that it can happen here. After all, if you grew up in the United States, you grew up in a country which has not had a serious economic depression since 1929. Perhaps you think that money problems are reserved for less developed countries like Mexico. Wrong! It could happen here because it is planned to happen here. And it is going to happen unless We the People do something now to change the system.

The reason that the system is about to collapse is debt. The total public and private debt is currently over $26 trillion. Dividing that up equally means that every man, woman, and child in the country is over $104,000 in debt. If we figure the cost of interest at 8%, it means that each of us pays more than $8,000 a year in interest. This cost is included in the price of every product and service that we buy.

As you know from the story about the missing dollar, the interest to pay off this debt was never placed into circulation. Therefore, there is no way that the national debt can be paid off. The situation was purposely created by a small cartel of international bankers who have made greed their god and power their aphrodisiac.

Even though these bankers seek to enslave the world through their fraudulent money and banking system, there is a way to peacefully evolve the system and put an end to the slavery.

THE JUBILEE YEAR

Beginning on July 26, 1995, people all around the world are going to begin using, alongside the current Gregorian calendar of 12 months, a lunar, Mayan calendar consisting of 13 months of 28 days each.

The idea of changing from the Gregorian calendar to the Mayan calendar is the work of José Argüelles, author of the book *The Mayan Factor.* José has pointed out that our current Gregorian calendar is out of harmony with the rhythm of the Universe. He has suggested that we would change our lives by moving back into the harmony of a calendar which is based on the cycles of the moon. Making this simple, fundamental change and altering the way we think about time and money could end the control of the international bankers.

José has pointed out that the concept that time equals money began in 1582 with the coming together of two events, the Edict of Pope Gregory XIII, which established our current calendar, and the invention of the mechanical watch, which divided time into a 12/60 time frequency. These two elements combined in our thinking until we began to equate time with money.

To change our thinking, to end the slavery, we may merely need to alter the way we measure time. July 26, 1995 is the first day of the Mayan year. It is also the first day of a Jubilee Year, a year in which We the People are to cancel all bank debts.

BANK DEBTS
FORGIVEN AND CANCELLED

I have included in this chapter a series of four letters that you can use to challenge your fraudulent credit card debts. The first three letters have been used with considerable success. (The fourth letter was put together by my staff and me. As we go to press, the fourth letter has not yet been tested.)

When you begin sending these letters out, the bank may not contact you again. Or, they may contact you by telephone or by letter. If they call, tell the person on the line that they are trying to collect a fraudulent debt and that you are putting them on notice. Ask the caller for his or her name, address, telephone, and social security number, and add, "so that my attorney can reach you." Keep a record of everything that is said. Insist that all future contact be made through the mail, and that all papers be signed "under penalty of perjury," explaining that you don't do your banking over the phone. If you have some uneasiness about canceling the debt rather than paying it off, ask yourself the following questions:

- ☞ Did the credit card company create money out of thin air? *Yes.*

- ☞ Did the credit card company lend you any money? *No.*

- ☞ If you pay back what the credit card company created in a matter of minutes with money that you earn through your labor, will you be cheated? *Yes.*

If canceling your credit card debt will *harm* no one, and paying off your credit card debt will *help* no one, (it will only allow the dishonesty of the bankers to continue), then the only one who stands to be harmed is you—if you choose to pay off the debt rather than cancel it.

If you are still feeling uneasy, remember this: The law is on your side. Creating money out of thin air is dishonest. In addition, the law allows you to collect up to triple damages when you catch a bank defrauding you. For example, if your card has a credit limit of $5,000, you could sue the bank for up to $15,000. And you may be entitled to recover all of the money that you have paid to the credit card company over the years, as well.

First Letter

Date
Certified Mail No.

Credit Card Company
Address
City, State, Zip

Dear Sir or Madam:

It has come to my attention that (credit card company) and other banks within the Federal Reserve System have been perpetrating a fraud on the American public. I have some questions which need to be answered before I continue to make payments on or use my (credit card company) card. My account number is (card number). The following are my questions:

1. Whose account did you withdraw money from in order to pay the vendors when I made charges to my account?

2. Was the money created by my signing the voucher when I made the purchase?

3. Is it (credit card company)'s policy to create checkbook money in amounts equal to the charges made by (credit card company) customers?

4. Does (credit card company) have on file a contract signed by me with a bona fide signature?

5. Will (credit card company) provide a copy of the journal entry that is made when I make a charge?

Please answer these questions within ten (10) days so that I am not late in making my payment. If I do not hear from you, I will assume that what I have heard is the truth and will, therefore, rescind my contract with (credit card company), as I do not wish to be a party to fraud.

Thank you, in advance, for your cooperation. I look forward to hearing from you so that I may dispel the rumors that I have heard.

Sincerely,

Your Name
C/o Your Street
Your City, Your State, Your Postal Zone
Without Prejudice UCC 1-207
(This letter was originally drafted by John Napieralski.)

Second Letter

Send this letter after ten days if you've received no response to the first letter. (Send with the Affidavit that follows.)

Date
Certified Mail No.

Credit Card Company
Address
City, State, Zip

Dear Sir or Madam:

I sent a letter on (date), a copy of which is attached, asking for information regarding how (credit card company) operates and how charges and the like are handled within its system. My questions remain unanswered, but I have done an enormous amount of research regarding these matters. (Credit card company) has refused to answer my questions, so I have taken this to mean that it is doing as other banks are, namely, loaning or creating credit on its books. I am withholding payment based on my letter of (date). If you can prove to me that your bank actually gave me or the vendors involved something other than an electronic entry using my charge as a deposit on your books in order to create an electronic deposit to the vendors' accounts (checkbook money), then I will be willing to pay the balance(s) due.

In addition to my original questions, I would also like you to provide the following information: 1) A copy of the bank charter, and 2) The names of all of the members of the Board of Directors.

I am in possession of a booklet published by the Federal Reserve Bank of Chicago called "Modern Money Mechanics." The booklet describes who creates money. The Court decision in <u>First National Bank of Montgomery</u> v <u>Jerome Daly</u> (1968 Minn. case; jury reached its verdict Dec. 7, 1968. Local case; did not go to appeal or Supreme Ct. Cite not found.) prohibits banks from creating money and credit upon their own books by means of book-ing entries. It is my belief that this is what you are doing and that this is fraud. I will not be a party to this fraud.

Please respond within ten (10) days with all of the information that I have requested. Unless I hear from you to the contrary, I will consider my accounts with you closed and this matter settled. Please be sure to sign any further correspondence under penalty of perjury and send it only to the address exactly as it appears below. Thank you, in advance, for your cooperation.

Sincerely,

Your Name
C/o Your Street
Your City, Your State, Your Postal Zone
Without Prejudice UCC 1-207

(See page 75 for the telephone number to call to obtain free copies of "Modern Money Mechanics.")

Affidavit of Revocation of Signature for Cause

This Affidavit is to be sent with the previous letter.
Point #5 requires you to fill in the
UCC Statutory Citation for your state.
Refer to example and chart on page 94.

1. Comes now Affiant having full, first-hand knowledge of the facts herein and, by making this affidavit of his own first-hand knowledge, affirms that the facts stated herein are true and correct to the best of his knowledge.

2. On or about (date you signed your credit card app.), Affiant signed documents without knowledge that a fraud was being perpetrated upon Affiant.

3. That Affiant was coerced into signing documents

without any knowledge that a fraud was being perpetrated upon Affiant.

4. That Affiant's revocation of signature constitutes a recission of signature. Thus, the contract no longer exists.

5. Affiant hereby revokes and makes void all signatures for cause as per UCC 3-501; (type in UCC Statutory Citation for your state. See page 94 for details).

6. Now Affiant is formally and timely removing the aforementioned signature(s) for all time and removing any nexus that (credit card company) may presume to have over Affiant by virtue of said signature(s).

_____ WITNESS:_____
(your name)   (name of witness)

_____ WITNESS:_____
(date)   (name of witness)

(This letter and Affidavit were originally drafted by John Napieralski.)

Third Letter

If, at this point, you receive a bill from the credit card company, send this letter.

Date
Certified Mail No.

Credit Card Company
Address
City, State, Zip

Dear Sir or Madam:

I am returning your correspondence, as this matter has been settled. Please see the attached copies of my letters of (dates). I have not received a response to these letters and, therefore, have concluded that (credit card company) is operating fraudulently and that it has not loaned me anything but a liability. Until you prove to me that your bank has advanced to me a bank asset, I am under no obligation to it whatsoever. (Credit card company) has not fulfilled its contract with me. I know that your bank's records still show that it owes me an asset because what (credit card company) loaned me was created by my note to them. If (credit card company) wants payment in like funds, then I will be glad to send you a promissory note, which is all that (credit card company) ever gave me.

I will consider this matter to be closed on your part also, unless (credit card company) answers my letters. Any further contact from you will be considered harassment and will be dealt with accordingly. If you find it necessary to contact me, please do so only at the address below, exactly as it appears. All other correspondence will be refused, and telephone calls will not be accepted. In addition, all further correspondence should be signed under penalty of perjury with the signature of a real person.

Sincerely,

Your Name
C/o Your Street
Your City, Your State, Your Postal Zone
Without Prejudice UCC 1-207

(This letter was originally drafted by John Napieralski.)

Fourth Letter
This letter is to be used in the event that you are threatened with collection.

Date
Certified Mail No.

Attn: Legal Department
Credit Card Company

Address
City, State, Zip

Dear Legal Department:

I am returning your credit card number (card number) and demanding proof of the cancellation of all of the related computer-generated bookkeeping entries. Failure on your part to cancel your computer records or any action by you or your agents to collect on this account will result in immediate reprisal.

This action is being taken and this refusal is made timely and for cause, pursuant to UCC 3-501—Refusal for Cause Without Dishonor; (state statute inserted here. See page 94).

UCC 3-501(b)(3) states:

"Without dishonoring the instrument, the party to whom presentment is made may (i) return the instrument for lack of a necessary endorsement, or (ii) refuse payment or acceptance for failure of the presentment to comply with the terms of the instrument, an agreement of the parties, or other applicable law or rule."

The reasons for my refusal are as follows:

Bank Fraud

When I first contracted for my credit card, I mistakenly thought that (credit card company) would be loaning me money which it received from other depositors and/or investors. Now I have found from reading "Modern Money Mechanics," which is published by the Federal Reserve Bank of Chicago, that (credit card company) created the money that I borrowed by using my promise to pay to generate computer entries on my account. In effect, your bank created money out of thin air.

In all of my transactions with (credit card company), you have failed to notify me that your bank created money out of thin air. Now that I have discovered this, I am prepared to proceed against (credit card company) for bank fraud. Your transaction with me lacked two of the necessary elements of a contract.

89

I am aware that the United States Code, Title 12, Section 24, Paragraph 7 confers upon a bank the power to lend its money, not its credit. In First National Bank of Tallapoosa v Monroe, 135 Ga 614; 69 S.E. 1123 (1911), the court, after citing the statute heretofore quoted, said, "[T]he provisions referred to do not give power to a national bank to guarantee the payment of the obligations of others solely for their benefit, nor is such power incidental of the business of banking. A bank can lend its money but not its credit."

In Howard & Foster Co. v Citizens National Bank of Union, 133 S.C. 202; 130 SE 758, (1927) it was said: "It has been settled beyond controversy that a national bank, under federal law, being limited in its power and capacity, cannot lend its credit by guaranteeing the debt of another. All such contracts being entered into by its officers are ultra vires and not binding upon the corporation. See also Merchants Bank of Valdosta v Baird, 160 F 642; 17 Lns 526 (1876).

(Credit card company) did not tell me that it was creating money out of thin air, called "bank credit," because to do so would have disclosed that there was no consideration from (credit card company) to me. "A lawful consideration must exist and be tendered to support the note." See Anheuser Busch Brewing Co. v Emma Mason, 44 Minn. 318, 46 NW 558 (1890). In short, if there is no full disclosure and no consideration, there is no contract.

Peonage

(Credit card company)'s manner of transacting business has made me a debt slave. This is in violation of the Thirteenth Amendment to the Constitution of the United States, which expressly forbids involuntary servitude. The United States Supreme Court addressed involuntary servitude, also called peonage, in Clyatt v U.S., 197 U.S. 207, 215-216; 25 S.Ct. 429; 49 L. Ed. 726 (1905), when it said:

"Peonage is sometimes classified as voluntary or involuntary, but this implies simply a difference in the mode of origin, but none of the character of the servitude. The one exists where the debtor voluntarily contracts to enter the service of his creditor.

The other is forced upon the debtor by some provision of law."

In addition, (credit card company)'s method of creating money out of thin air and charging interest upon the transaction is a violation of the Biblical law of "just weights and measures." (Credit card company) is able to create money in moments that will take me years of labor to pay off. (Credit card company) has made me a slave by debt, controlling my time by loaning me "bank credit" in the place of money.

Let the record reflect that I no longer consent to accepting (credit card company)'s demands upon me for my money. Your manner of conducting business is in direct violation of the laws of God, the laws of contracts, the Constitution of the United States of America, and my civil rights.

Revocation of Signature

By refusing (credit card company)'s statement in a timely manner according to UCC 3-501, I hereby revoke my signature on the original application as presented to (credit card company). The original application was fraudulent on its face, as it did not provide full disclosure. The document did not say that (credit card company) was going to loan me "bank credit" which it created out of thin air.

Had (credit card company) disclosed to me that I was borrowing "bank credit," I would have known that the element of consideration was missing from the contract.

It is a well-established principal of law that fraud has no statute of limitations and that its presence cancels every agreement. I demand that you cancel our agreement and return to me every dollar of my labor, plus any interest that I have ever paid to you.

Conspiracy

How you and your fellow bankers have been allowed to cheat the American public for so long can only be explained by the knowledge that the Federal Reserve Banks are privately owned and operated for profit. For all practical purposes, because of your interlocking activities and practices, all banks in this country are in the law to be treated as one and the same bank because each bank in the system is obligated to accept the checks of other member banks as if they were issued by itself. (Credit card company) has been able to transfer my labor to its balance sheet by entering bookkeeping entries into its computer.

NOTICE

UCC 3-503 allows you thirty (30) days from receipt of this Refusal for Cause Without Dishonor to state under oath the following: That (credit card company) did not create money by loaning its credit and charging interest upon that loan, in violation of the law of contracts.

If you do not respond within thirty (30) days, a default will be created through material misrepresentation which will vitiate anything that occurred from the time that we began doing business together until thirty (30) days from now. UCC 1-103.

If, within thirty (30) days, you do not either answer to the above under oath or provide me with proof of the cancellation of this computer-generated debt, the return of my application, and the return of all monies that I have paid to you since the beginning of our business relationship, then I will seek damages for fraud. The Uniform Commercial Code allows me to seek the return of all monies paid to (credit card company) plus triple damages.

Guard yourselves accordingly.

Sincerely,

Your Name
c/o Your Street
Your City, Your State, Your Postal Zone
Without Prejudice UCC 1-207

MORTGAGES FORGIVEN AND CANCELLED

Once your credit card debt has been forgiven, it will be time to move on to your mortgage(s). Because of the amount of money involved in canceling your mortgage, the bankers will resist. So, when you cancel your mortgage, expect to end up in court. But, by the time you are ready to cancel your mortgage, there will be many who will have gone before you, and the road will be well traveled. If you need some help with the paperwork, contact us at De-Taxing America for support. We will be glad to work with you or your attorney.

THE NATIONAL DEBT

Picture millions of us canceling and banks forgiving our fraudulent bank debts. Imagine the impact that this would have on Congress. It would send a clear message that We the People understand the fraudulent nature of the national debt. Without a national debt, there would be little or no need for an individual income tax. The I.R.S. would then be scaled back to collecting only those taxes which are constitutionally correct.

THE CHOICE

The time for change is NOW. The choice before us is this: Will We the People bring the changes about or will the bankers be allowed to complete their plans for a New World Order?

The best way I know to change the system is to exit the system by canceling our fraudulent bank debts. History teaches that slaves cannot be freed. Slaves must free themselves. And they will free themselves when they have had enough. I have had enough. Have you?

UNIFORM COMMERCIAL CODE

The fifth point on the Affidavit of Revocation of Signature for Cause requires you to fill in the UCC Statutory Citation for your state.

For example:
5. Affiant hereby revokes and makes void all signatures for cause as per UCC 3-501; (type in the UCC Statutory Citation for your state).

If you are from California you should type:
5. Affiant hereby revokes and makes void all signatures for cause as per UCC 3-501; West's Ann.Cal.Com. Code, Sub. Sec. 3501

Use the following chart to find your state's citation.

Table of Jurisdictions Wherein Code Has Been Adopted

Jurisdiction	Statutory Citation
Alabama	Code 1975, Sub. Sec. 7-3-501
Alaska	refer to specific state statute found at AS Sub Sec 45.01 et seq.
Arizona	A.R.S. Sub. Sec. 47-3501
Arkansas	A.C.A. Sub. Sec. 4-3-501
California	West's Ann.Cal.Com.Code, Sub. Sec. 3501
Colorado	West's C.R.S.A. Sub. Sec. 4-3-501
Connecticut	C.G.S.A. Sub. Sec. 42a-3-501
Delaware	6 Del.C. Sub. Sec. 3-5-1
Dist. of Columbia	D.C.Code 1981, Sub. Sec. 28:3-501

Florida .... refer to specific state statute found at West's F.S.A. Sub. Sec. 670.101 et seq.

Georgia .... O.C.G.A. Sub. Sec. 11-3-501

Guam .... 13 G.C.A. Sub. Sec. 3501

Hawaii .... HRS Sub. Sec. 490:3-501

Idaho .... I.C. Sub. Sec. 28-3-501

Illinois .... S.H.A. 810 ILCS 5/3-501

Indiana .... West's A.I.C. 26-1-3-501

Iowa .... I.C.A. Sub. Sec. 554.3501

Kansas .... K.S.A. 84-3-501

Kentucky .... KRS 355.3-501

Louisiana .... LSA-R.S. 10:3-501

Maine .... 11 M.R.S.A. Sub. Sec. 3-501

Maryland .... Code, Commercial Law, Sub. Sec. 3-501

Massachusetts .... M.G.L.A. c. 106, Sub. Sec. 3-501

Michigan .... M.C.L.A. Sub. Sec. 440.3501(3)

Minnesota .... M.S.A. Sub. Sec. 336.3-501

Mississippi .... Code 1972, Sub. Sec. 75-3-501

Missouri .... V.A.M.S. Sub. Sec. 400.3-501

Montana .... MCA 30-3-501

Nebraska .... Neb.U.C.C. Sub. Sec. 3-501

Nevada .... N.R.S. 104.3501

New Hampshire .... RSA 382-A:3-501

New Jersey .... N.J.S.A. 12 A:3-501

New Mexico .... NMSA 1978, Sub. Sec. 55-3-501

New York .... McKinney's Uniform Commercial Code, Sub. Sec. 3-501

North Carolina .... G.S. Sub. Sec. 25-3-501

North Dakota .... refer to specific state statute found at NDCC 41-01-02 et seq.

Ohio .... refer to specific state statute found at R.C. Sub. Sec. 1301.01 et seq.

Oklahoma .... 12A Okl.St.Ann. Sub. Sec. 3-501

Oregon .... ORS 71.3501

Pennsylvania .... 13 Pa.C.S.A. Sub. Sec. 3501

Rhode Island .... Gen.Laws 1956, Sub. Sec. 6A-3-501

South Carolina .... Code 1976, Sub. Sec. 36-3-501

South Dakota .... SDCL 57A-3-501

Tennessee .... T.C.A. Sub. Sec. 47-3-501

Texas .... V.T.C.A., Bus. & C. Sub. Sec. 3.501

Utah U.C.A.1953, 70A-3-501

Vermont .... 9A V.S.A. Sub. Sec. 3-501

Virgin Islands .... 11A V.I.C. Sub. Sec. 3-501

Virginia .... Code 1950, Sub. Sec. 8:3-501

Washington .... West's RCWA 62A.3-501

West Virginia .... Code, 46-3-501

Wisconsin .... W.S.A. 403.501

Wyoming .... W.S.1977, Sub. Sec. 34.1-3-501

BOOKS VIDEOS TRANSCRIPTS

BOOKS

THE BEST KEPT SECRET
by Otto Skinner

This book provides the clearest explanation of the "income tax" and the so-called Sixteenth Amendment available today. Find out why an employee is not subject to any tax withholdings, including the "Social Security" tax, unless the nature of the employee's job involves an activity that cannot be pursued as a matter of constitutional right. The free exercise of a constitutionally-secured right cannot be, and therefore has not been, taxed for revenue purposes. Cost **$15.95.**

I.R.S. HUMBUG—I.R.S. Weapons of Enslavement
by Frank Kowalik

The I.R.S. tells us, through Frank Kowalik's experience, that you do not pay them taxes, but rather that you discharge either a legal or illegal kickback. Federal government employee humbug (meaning hoax with intent to deceive) and how to make a defense is revealed in this hardcover, 365-page book.

From the study of "I.R.S. Humbug" you will learn that you have the "right" to refuse to accept the tax collector's service, which is subject to voluntary compliance, that you are not the "taxpayer" under the Internal Revenue Code, and much more. Cost **$29.95.**

IF YOU ARE THE DEFENDANT
by Otto Skinner

This book provides an in-depth, yet very clear explanation of why there can be no intelligent discussion and no adequate defense until all parties concerned clearly understand today's so-called indirect excise tax. Cost **$19.95.**

THE FEDERAL MAFIA—How It Illegally Imposes and Unlawfully Collects Income Taxes.
by Irwin Schiff

This book reveals, in shocking detail, how every aspect of the federal income tax is implemented in violation of the law and the U.S. Constitution. You will discover, among other things, that no law requires you to file an income tax return or to pay this tax. Cost **$23.95.**

97

VULTURES IN EAGLE'S CLOTHING
by Lynne Meredith

This impeccably researched book is a poignant exposé of the I.R.S.'s most closely guarded secrets. With both truth and Supreme Court rulings, it proves the federal income tax to be voluntary while empowering the reader with knowledge of procedures used to volunteer OUT of the system. Also contains the inspiring stories of citizens who have received letters from the I.R.S. saying they are no longer required to file a tax return. Cost **$39.95.**

ROBOT'S REBELLION
by David Icke

People of all nations have allowed themselves to be programmed by the ideas which those in power have fed to them. David Icke tears down the veils of hypocrisy built up for generations by the corrupt forces of Church, State, science, and commerce.

He also points to the frightening influence wielded throughout the planet by a merciless and manipulative network of secret societies. Long-established links between certain groups have been suppressed for years by the world's power-broking hierarchy. Cost **$14.95.**

ANTI-SHYSTER Commercial Lien Study Guide
by Alfred Adask
Cost **$34.95.**

INTERNAL REVENUE CODE BOOK 1 & 2
Cost **$65.00** per set.

VIDEOS

LIBERTY IN THE BALANCE—America, the FED, and the I.R.S.

Learn the history of the Federal Reserve, the I.R.S., and the income tax, as well as how America has been deceived, who is behind the corruption, and what you can do about it. THIS VIDEO EXPOSES ALL! THIS IS A MUST! Cost **$24.95.**

THE BUCK ACT

Beginning with a single unconstitutional act, the federal government has spread out from Washington, D.C. to meddle in every aspect of our lives. By knowing the source of the government's manipulations, you can stand up and say, "No," and be on firm ground. A companion to "Liberty in the Balance." Cost **$24.95.**

TRANSCRIPTS

LLOYD LONG TRIAL TRANSCRIPT

Found "Not Guilty" by a jury of his peers, Lloyd Long has put future litigation by the I.R.S. in serious jeopardy. This is a great bedtime novel for those considering standing up to the I.R.S. In 400 pages, you'll have it all. Cost **$45.95.**

THE GREAT
SNOW JOB

PART III

THE DECLARATION
OF INDEPENDENCE
THE CONSTITUTION
THE BILL OF RIGHTS

The Declaration of Independence
IN CONGRESS, JULY 4, 1776
The unanimous Declaration of the thirteen United States of America

When in the course of human events, it becomes necessary for one people to dissolve the political bands which have connected them with one another, and to assume among the powers of the Earth, the separate and equal station to which the laws of nature and of nature's God entitle them, a decent respect to the opinions of mankind requires that they should declare the causes which impel them to the separation.

We hold these truths to be self-evident, that all men are created equal, that they are endowed by their Creator with certain unalienable rights, that among these are life, liberty and the pursuit of happiness.— That to secure these rights, governments are instituted among men, deriving their just powers from the consent of the governed.— That whenever any form of government becomes destructive of these ends, it is the right of the people to alter or to abolish it, and to institute new government, laying its foundation on such principles and organizing its powers in such form, as to them shall deem most likely to effect their safety and happiness. Prudence, indeed, will dictate that governments long established should not be changed for light and transient causes; and accordingly all experience hath shown, that mankind are more disposed to suffer, while evils are sufferable, than to right themselves by abolishing the forms to which they are accustomed. But when a long train of abuses and usurpations, pursuing invariably the same object evinces a design to reduce them under absolute despotism, it is their right, it is their duty, to throw off such government, and to provide new guards for their future security.—

Such has been the patient sufferance of these Colonies; and such is now the necessity which constrains them to alter their former systems of government. The history of the present King of Great Britain is a history of repeated injuries and usurpations, all having in direct object the establishment of an absolute tyranny over these States. To prove this, let facts be submitted to a candid world.

He has refused his assent to laws, the most wholesome and necessary for the public good.

He has forbidden his Governors to pass laws, of immediate and pressing importance, unless suspended in their operation till his assent should be obtained; and when so suspended, he has utterly neglected to attend to them.

He has refused to pass other laws for the accommodation of large districts of people, unless those people would relinquish the right of representation in the legislature, a right inestimable to them and formidable to tyrants only.

He has called together legislative bodies at places unusual, uncomfortable, and distant from the depository of their public records, for the sole purpose of fatiguing them into compliance with his measures.

He has dissolved representative houses repeatedly, for opposing with manly firmness his invasion on the rights of the people.

He has refused for a long time, after such dissolutions to cause others to be elected; whereby the legislative powers, incapable of annihilation, have returned to the people at large for their exercise; the State remaining in the mean time exposed to all the dangers of invasion from without, and convulsions within.

He has endeavored to prevent the population of these States; for that purpose obstructing the laws for naturalization of foreigners; refusing to pass others to encourage their migrations hither, and raising the conditions of new appropriations of lands.

He has obstructed the administration of justice, by refusing his assent to laws for establishing judiciary powers.

He has made judges dependent on his Will alone, for the tenure of their offices, and the amount and payment of their salaries.

He has erected a multitude of new offices, and sent hither swarms of officers to harass our people, and eat out their substance.

He has kept among us, in times of peace, standing armies without the consent of our legislatures.—

He has affected to render the military independent of and superior to the civil power.

He has combined with others to subject us to a jurisdiction foreign to our constitution, and unacknowledged by our laws; giving his assent to their actions of pretended legislation:—

For quartering large bodies of armed troops among us:

For protecting them, by a mock trial, from punishment for any murders which they should commit on the inhabitants of these States:

For cutting off our trade with all parts of the world:

For imposing taxes on us without our consent:

For depriving us in many cases, of the benefits of trial by jury:

For transporting us beyond seas to be tried for pretended offenses:

For abolishing the free system of English laws in a neighboring province, establishing therein an arbitrary government, and enlarging its boundaries so as to render it at once an example and fit instrument for introducing the same absolute rule into these Colonies:

For taking away our charters, abolishing our most valuable laws, and altering fundamentally the forms of our governments.

For suspending our own legislatures, and declaring themselves invested with power to legislate for us in all cases whatsoever.

He has abdicated government here, by declaring us out of his protection and waging war against us.

He has plundered our seas, ravaged our coasts, burnt our towns, and destroyed the lives of our people.

He is at this time transporting large armies of foreign mercenaries to complete the works of death, desolation and tyranny, already begun with circumstances of cruelty and perfidy scarcely paralleled in the most barbarous ages, and totally unworthy the head of a civilized nation.

He has constrained our fellow citizens taken captive on the high seas to bear arms against their country, to become the executioners of their friends and brethren, or to fall themselves by their hands.

He has excited domestic insurrections amongst us, and has endeavored to bring on the inhabitants of our frontiers, the merciless Indian savages, whose known rule of warfare, is an undistinguished destruction of all ages, sexes and conditions.

In every stage of these oppressions We have petitioned for redress in the most humble terms: Our repeated petitions have been answered only by repeated injury. A prince, whose character is thus marked by every act which may define a tyrant, is unfit to be the ruler of a free people.

Nor have We been wanting in attentions to our British brethren. We have warned them from time to time of attempts by their legislature to extend an unwarrantable jurisdiction over us. We have reminded them of the circumstances of our emigration and settlement here. We appealed to their native justice and magnanimity, and we have conjured them by the ties of our common kindred to disavow these usurpations, which, would inevitably interrupt our connections and correspondence. They too have been deaf to the voice of justice and consanguinity. We must, therefore, acquiesce in the necessity, which denounces our separation, and hold them, as we hold the rest of mankind, enemies in war, in peace friends.

We, therefore, the Representatives of the United States of America, in General Congress, assembled, appealing to the Supreme Judge of the World for the rectitude of our intentions, do, in the name, and by the authority of the good people of these Colonies, solemnly publish and declare, that these United Colonies are, and of right ought to be free and independent states; that they are absolved from all allegiance to the British Crown, and that all political connection between them and the State of Great Britain, is and ought to be totally dissolved; and that as free and independent states, they have full power to levy war, conclude peace, contract alliances, establish commerce, and to do all other acts and things which independent states may of right do.

And for the support of this Declaration, with a firm reliance on the protection of divine providence, we mutually pledge to each other our lives, our fortunes and our sacred honor.

The Constitution

Preamble
We the People of the United States, in Order to form a more perfect Union, establish justice, insure domestic tranquillity, provide for the common defence, promote the general welfare, and secure the blessings of liberty to ourselves and our posterity, do ordain and establish this Constitution for the United States of America.

Article I

Section 1. All legislative Powers herein granted shall be vested in a Congress of the United States, which shall consist of a Senate and House of Representatives.

Section 2. The House of Representatives shall be composed of members chosen every second year by the people of the several States, and the electors in each State shall have the qualifications requisite for electors of the most numerous branch of the State Legislature.

No person shall be a Representative who shall not have attained to the age of twenty-five years, and been seven years a citizen of the United States, and who shall not, when elected, be an inhabitant of that State in which he shall be chosen.

Representatives and direct taxes shall be apportioned among the several States which may be included within this Union, according to their respective numbers, which shall be determined by adding to the whole number of free persons, including those bound to service for a term of years, and excluding Indians not taxed, three-fifths of all other persons. The actual enumeration shall be made within three years after the first meeting of the Congress of the United States, and within every subsequent term of ten years, in such manner as they by law shall direct. The number of representatives shall not exceed one for every thirty thousand, but each State shall have at least one Representative;

and until such enumeration shall be made, the State of New Hampshire shall be entitled to choose three; Massachusetts eight; Rhode Island and Providence Plantations one; Connecticut five; New York six; New Jersey four; Pennsylvania eight; Delaware one; Maryland six; Virginia ten; North Carolina five; South Carolina five; and Georgia three.

When vacancies happen in the representation from any State, the executive authority thereof shall issue Writs of election to fill such vacancies.

The House of Representatives shall choose their Speaker and other officers; and shall have the sole power of impeachment.

Section 3. The senate of the United States shall be composed of two Senators from each State, chosen by the legislature thereof, for six years; and each Senator shall have one vote.

Immediately after they shall be assembled in consequence of the first election, they shall be divided as equally as may be into three classes. The seats of the Senators of the first class shall be vacated at the expiration of the second year, of the second class at the expiration of the fourth year, and of the third class at the expiration of the sixth year, so that one third may be chosen every second year; and if vacancies happen by resignation, or otherwise, during the recess of the legislature of any State, the executive thereof may make temporary appointments until the next meeting of the legislature, which shall then fill such vacancies.

No person shall be a Senator who shall not have attained to the age of thirty years, and been nine years a citizen of the United States, and who shall not, when elected, be an inhabitant of the State for which he shall be chosen.

The Vice President of the United States shall be president of the Senate, but shall have no vote, unless they be equally divided.

The Senate shall choose their other officers, and also a president pro tempore, in the absence of the Vice President, or when he shall exercise the office of President of the United States.

The Senate shall have the sole power to try all impeachments. When sitting for that purpose, they shall be on oath or affirmation. When the President of the United States is tried, the Chief Justice shall preside; and no person shall be convicted without the concurrence of two-thirds of the members present.

Judgment in cases of impeachment shall not extend further than to removal from office, and disqualification to hold and enjoy any office of honor, trust or profit under the United States: but the party convicted shall nevertheless be liable and subject to indictment, trial, judgment and punishment, according to Law.

Section 4. The times, places and manner of holding elections for Senators and Representatives, shall be prescribed in each State by the Legislature thereof; but the Congress may at any time by law make or alter such regulations, except as to the places of choosing Senators.

The Congress shall assemble at least once in every year, and such meeting shall be on the first Monday in December, unless they shall by law appoint a different day.

Section 5. Each house shall be the judge of the elections, returns and qualifications of its own members, and a majority of each shall constitute a quorum to do business, but a smaller number may adjourn from day to day, and may be authorized to compel the attendance of absent members, in such manner, and under such penalties as each House may provide.

Each House may determine the rules of its proceedings, punish its members for disorderly behavior, and, with the concurrence of two-thirds, expel a member.

Each House shall keep a journal of its proceedings, and from time to time publish the same, excepting such parts as may in their judgment require secrecy; and the yeas and nays of the members of either house on any question shall, at the desire of one-fifth of those present, be entered on the journal.

Neither House, during the session of Congress, shall, without the consent of the other, adjourn for more than three days, nor to any other place than that in which the two Houses shall be sitting.

Section 6. The Senators and Representatives shall receive a compensation for their services, to be ascertained by law, and paid out of the Treasury of the United States. They shall in all cases, except treason, felony, and breach of the peace, be privileged from arrest during their attendance at the session of their respective Houses, and in going to and returning from the same; and for any speech or debate in either House, they shall not be questioned in any other place.

No Senator or Representatives shall, during the time for which he was elected, be appointed to any civil office under the authority of the United States, which shall have been created, or the emoluments whereof shall have been increased during such time; and no person holding any office under the United States, shall be a member of either House during his continuance in office.

Section 7. All bills for raising revenue shall originate in the House of

Representatives; but the Senate may propose or concur with amendments as on other bills.

Every bill which shall have passed the House of Representatives and the Senate, shall, before it becomes a law, be presented to the President of the United States; if he approves he shall sign it, but if not he shall return it, with his objections to that House in which it shall have originated, who shall enter the objections at large on the journal, and proceed to reconsider it. If after such reconsideration two-thirds of that House shall agree to pass the bill, it shall be sent, together with the objections, to the other House, by which it shall likewise be reconsidered, and if approved by two-thirds of that House, it shall become a law. But in all such cases the votes of both Houses shall be determined by yeas and nays, and the names of the persons voting for and against the bill shall be entered on the journal of each House respectively. If any bill shall not be returned by the President within ten days (Sundays excepted) after it shall have been presented to him, the same shall be a law, in like manner as if he had signed it, unless the Congress by their adjournment prevent its return, in which case it shall not be a law.

Every order, resolution, or vote to which the concurrence of the Senate and House of Representatives may be necessary (except on a question of adjournment) shall be presented to the President of the United States; and before the same shall take effect, shall be approved by him, or being disapproved by him, shall be repassed by two-thirds of the Senate and House of Representatives, according to the rules and limitations prescribed in the case of a bill.

Section 8. The Congress shall have power to lay and collect taxes, duties, imposts and excises, to pay the debts and provide for the common defence and general welfare of the United States; but all duties, imposts and excises shall be uniform throughout the United States;

To borrow money on the credit of the United States;

To regulate commerce with foreign nations, and among the several States, and with the Indian tribes;

To establish an uniform rule of naturalization, and uniform laws on the subject of bankruptcies throughout the United States;

To coin money, regulate the value thereof, and of foreign coin, and fix the standard of weights and measures;

To provide for the punishment of counterfeiting the securities and current coin of the United States;

To establish post offices and post roads;

To promote the progress of science and useful arts, by securing for limited times to authors and inventors the exclusive right to their respective writings and discoveries;

To constitute tribunals inferior to the Supreme Court;

To define and punish piracies and felonies committed on the high seas, and offenses against the laws of the nations;

To declare war, grant letters of marque and reprisal, and make rules concerning captures on land and water;

To raise and support armies, but no appropriation of money to that use shall be for a longer term than two years;

To provide and maintain a navy;

To make rules for the government and regulation of the land and naval forces;

To provide for calling forth the militia to execute the laws of the union, suppress insurrections, and repel invasions;

To provide for organizing, arming, and disciplining the militia, and for governing such part of them as may be employed in the service of the United States, reserving to the States respectively, the appointment of the officers, and the authority of training the militia according to the discipline prescribed by Congress.

To exercise exclusive legislation in all cases whatsoever, over such district (not exceeding ten miles square) as may, by cession of particular states, and the acceptance of Congress, become the seat of the Government of the United States, and to exercise like authority over all places purchased by the consent of the legislature of the State in which the same shall be, for the erection of forts, magazines, arsenals, dockyards, and other needful buildings;—And

To make all laws which shall be necessary and proper for carrying into execution the foregoing powers, and all other powers vested by this Constitution in the government of the United States, or in any department or office thereof.

Section 9. The migration or importation of such persons as any of the States now existing shall think proper to admit, shall not be prohibited by the Congress prior to the year one thousand eight hundred and eight, but a tax or duty may be imposed on such Importation, not exceeding ten dollars for each person.

The privilege of the writ of habeas corpus shall not be suspended, unless when in cases of rebellion or invasion, the public safety may require it.

No Bill of Attainder or ex post facto Law shall be passed.

No capitation, or other direct tax shall be laid, unless in proportion to the census or enumeration herein before directed to be taken.

No tax or duty shall be laid on articles exported from any state.

No preference shall be given by any regulation of commerce or revenue to the ports of one State over those of another; nor shall vessels bound to, or from, one State, be obliged to enter, clear, or pay duties in another.

No money shall be drawn from the Treasury, but in consequence of appropriations made by law; and a regular statement and account of the receipts and expenditures of all public money shall be published from time to time.

No title of nobility shall be granted by the United States; and no person holding any office of profit or trust under them shall, without the consent of the Congress, accept of any present, emolument, office, or title, of any kind whatever, from any King, Prince, or foreign State.

Section 10. No State shall enter into any treaty, alliance or confederation; grant Letters of Marque and Reprisal; coin money; emit Bills of Credit; make any thing but gold and silver coin a tender in payment of debts; pass any Bill of Attainder, ex post facto Law, or law impairing the obligation of contracts, or grant any title of nobility.

No State shall, without the consent of Congress, lay any imposts or duties on imports or exports, except what may be absolutely necessary for executing its inspection laws; and the net produce of all duties and imposts, laid by any State on imports or exports, shall be for the use of the Treasury of the United States; and all such laws shall be subject to the revision and control of the Congress.

No State shall, without the consent of Congress, lay any duty of tonnage, keep troops, or ships of war in time of peace, enter into any agreement or compact with another State, or with a foreign power, or engage in war, unless actually invaded, or in such imminent danger as will not admit of delay.

ARTICLE II

Section 1. The executive power shall be vested in a President of the United States of America. He shall hold his office during the term of four years, and, together with the Vice President, chosen for the same term, be elected, as follows:

Each State shall appoint, in such manner as the legislature thereof may direct, a number of electors, equal to the whole number of Senators and Representatives to which the State may be entitled in the Congress; but no Senator or Representative, or person holding an office of trust or profit under the United States, shall be appointed an elector.

The electors shall meet in their respective States, and vote by ballot for two persons, of whom one at least shall not be an inhabitant of the same State with themselves. And they shall make a list of all the persons voted for, and of the number of votes for each; which list they shall sign and certify, and transmit sealed to the seat of the Government of the United States, directed to the president of the Senate. The president of the Senate shall, in the presence of the Senate and House of Representatives, open all the certificates, and the votes shall then be counted. The person having the greatest number of votes shall be the President, if such number be a majority of the whole number of electors appointed; and if there be more than one who have such majority, and have an equal number of votes, then the House of Representatives, shall immediately choose by ballot one of them for President; and if no person have a majority, then from the five highest on the list the said House shall in like manner choose the President. But in choosing the President, the votes shall be taken by States, the representation from each State having one vote; A quorum for this purpose shall consist of a member, or members, from two thirds of the States, and a majority of all the States shall be necessary to a choice. In every case, after the choice of the President, the person having the greatest number of votes of the electors shall be the Vice President. But if there should remain two or more who have equal votes, the Senate shall choose from them by ballot the Vice President.

The Congress may determine the time of choosing the electors, and the day on which they shall give their votes; which day shall be the same throughout the United States.

No person except a natural born citizen, or a citizen of the United States, at the time of the adoption of this Constitution, shall be eligible to the office of President; neither shall any person be eligible to that office who shall not have attained to the age of thirty-five years, and been fourteen years a resident within the United States.

In case of the removal of the President from office, or of his death, resignation, or inability to discharge the powers and duties of the said office, the same shall devolve on the Vice President, and the Congress may by law provide for the case of removal, death, resignation or inability, both of the President and Vice President, declaring what officer shall then act as President, and such officer shall act accordingly, until the disability be removed, or a President shall be elected.

The President shall, at stated times, receive for his services, a compensation, which shall neither be increased nor diminished during the period for which he shall have been elected, and he shall not receive within that period any other emolument from the United States, or any of them.

Before he enter on the execution of his office, he shall take the following oath or affirmation:— "I do solemnly swear (or affirm) that I will faithfully execute the office of President of the United States, and will to the best of my ability, preserve, protect, and defend the Constitution of the United States."

Section 2. The President shall be Commander in Chief of the Army and Navy of the United States, and of the militia of the several States, when called into the actual service of the United States; he may require the opinion, in writing, of the principal officer in each of the executive departments, upon any subject relating to the duties of their respective offices, and he shall have power to grant reprieves and pardons for offenses against the United States, except in cases of impeachment.

He shall have power, by and with the advice and consent of the Senate, to make treaties; provided two-thirds of the Senators present concur; and he shall nominate, and by and with the advice and consent of the Senate, shall appoint ambassadors, other public ministers and consuls, Judges of the Supreme Court, and all other officers of the United States, whose appointments are not herein otherwise provided for, and which shall be established by law; but the Congress may by law vest the appointment of such inferior officers, as they think proper, in the President alone, in the courts of law, or in the heads of departments.

The President shall have power to fill up all vacancies that may happen during the recess of the Senate, by granting commissions which shall expire at the end of their next session.

Section 3. He shall from time to time give to the Congress information of the State of the Union, and recommend to their consideration such measures as he shall judge necessary and expedient; he may, on extraordinary occasions, convene both Houses, or either of them, and in case of disagreement between them, with respect to the time of adjournment, he may adjourn them to such time as he shall think proper; he shall receive ambassadors and other public ministers; he shall take care that the laws be faithfully executed, and shall commission all the officers of the United States.

Section 4. The President, Vice President and all civil officers of the United States, shall be removed from office on impeachment for and conviction of, treason, bribery, or other high crimes and misdemeanors.

ARTICLE III

Section 1. The judicial power of the United States, shall be vested in one Supreme Court, and in such inferior courts as the Congress may from time to time ordain and establish. The judges, both of the Supreme and inferior courts, shall hold their offices during good behavior, and shall, at stated times, receive for their services, a compensation, which shall not be diminished during their continuance in office.

Section 2. The judicial power shall extend to all cases, in law and equity, arising under this Constitution, the laws of the United States, and treaties made, or which shall be made, under their authority;—to all cases affecting ambassadors, other public ministers and consuls;—to all cases of admiralty and maritime jurisdiction;—to controversies to which the United States shall be a party;—to controversies between two or more States;—between a State and citizens of another State;—between citizens of different States;—between citizens of the same State claiming lands under grants of different States, and between a State, or the citizens thereof, and foreign States, citizens or subjects.

In all cases affecting ambassadors, other public ministers and consuls, and those in which a State shall be party, the Supreme Court shall have original jurisdiction. In all the other cases before mentioned, the Supreme Court shall have appellate jurisdiction, both as to law and fact, with such exceptions, and under such regulations as the Congress shall make.

The trial of all crimes, except in cases of impeachment, shall be by jury; and such trial shall be held in the State where the said crimes shall have been committed; but when not committed within any State, the trial shall be at such place or places as the Congress may by law have directed.

Section 3. Treason against the United States, shall consist only in levying war against them, or in adhering to their enemies, giving them aid and comfort. No person shall be convicted of treason unless on the testimony of two witnesses to the same overt act, or on confession in open court.

The Congress shall have power to declare the punishment of treason, but no attainder of treason shall work corruption of blood, or forfeiture except during the life of the person attained.

ARTICLE IV

Section 1. Full faith and credit shall be given in each State to the public acts, records, and judicial proceedings of every other State. And the Congress may by general laws prescribe the manner in which such acts, records, and proceedings shall be proved, and the effect thereof.

Section 2. The Citizens of each State shall be entitled to all privileges and immunities of citizens in the several States.

A person charged in any State with treason, felony, or other crime, who shall flee from justice, and be found in another State, shall on demand of the executive authority of the State from which he fled, be delivered up, to be removed to the State having jurisdiction of the crime.

No person held to service or labor in one State, under the laws thereof, escaping into another, shall in consequence of any law or regulation therein, be discharged from such service or labor, but shall be delivered up on claim of the party to whom such service or labor be due.

Section 3. New States may be admitted by the Congress into this Union; but no new State shall be formed or erected within the jurisdiction of any other State; nor any State be formed by the junction of two or more States, or parts of States, without the consent of the legislatures of the States concerned as well as of the Congress.

The Congress shall have power to dispose of and make all needful rules and regulations respecting the territory or other property belonging to the United States; and nothing in this Constitution shall be so construed as to prejudice any claims of the United States, or of any particular State.

Section 4. The United States shall guarantee to every State in this union a republican form of government, and shall protect each of them against invasion; and on application of the legislature, or of the executive (when the legislature cannot be convened) against domestic violence.

ARTICLE V

The Congress, whenever two-thirds of both Houses shall deem it necessary, shall propose amendments to this Constitution, or on the application of the legislatures of two-thirds of the several States, shall call a convention for proposing amendments, which, in either case, shall be valid to all intents and purposes, as part of this Constitution, when ratified by the legislatures of three-fourths of the several States, or by conventions in three-fourths thereof, as the one or the other mode of ratification may be proposed by the Congress; provided that no amendment which may be made prior to the year one thousand eight hundred and eight shall in any manner affect the first and fourth clauses in the Ninth Section of the First Article; and that no State, without its consent, shall be deprived of its equal suffrage in the Senate.

ARTICLE VI

All debts contracted and engagements entered into, before the adoption of this Constitution, shall be as valid against the United States under this Constitution, as under the Confederation.

This Constitution, and the laws of the United States which shall be made in pursuance thereof; and all treaties made, or which shall be made, under the authority of the United States, shall be the supreme law of the land; and the judges in every State shall be bound thereby, any thing in the Constitution or laws of any State to the contrary notwithstanding.

The Senators and Representatives before mentioned, and the members of the several State legislatures, and all executive and judicial officers, both of the United States and of the several States, shall be bound by oath or affirmation, to support this Constitution; but no religious test shall ever be required as the qualification to any office or public trust under the United States.

ARTICLE VII

The ratification of the conventions of nine States, shall be sufficient for the establishment of the Constitution between the States so ratifying the same.

Done in convention by the unanimous consent of the States present the seventeenth day of September in the year of our Lord one thousand seven hundred and eighty seven and of the independence of the United States of America the twelfth. In witness whereof we have hereunto subscribed our names.

George Washington-President
and deputy from Virginia

New Hampshire, John Langdon, Nicholas Gilman

Massachusetts, Nathaniel Gorham, Rufus King

Connecticut, William Samuel Johnson, Roger Sherman

New York, Alexander Hamilton

New Jersey, William Livingston, David Brearley, William Paterson, Jonathan Dayton

Virginia, John Blair, James Madison, Jr.

North Carolina, William Blount, Richard Dobbs Spaight, Hugh Williamson

Pennsylvania, Benjamin Franklin, Thomas Mifflin, Robert Morris, George Clymer, Thomas FitzSimons, Jared Ingersoll, James Wilson, Gouvernueur Morris

Delaware, Geofrey Read, Gunning Bedford Jr., John Dickinson, Richard Bassett, Jacob Broom

Maryland, James McHenry, Daniel of St. Thomas' Jenifer, Daniel Carroll

South Carolina, John Rutledge, Charles Cotesworth Pinckney, Charles Pinckney, Pierce Butler

Georgia, William Few, Abraham Baldwin

Attest: William Jackson, Secretary

IN CONVENTION
Monday September 17th, 1787
Present

The States of New Hampshire, Massachusetts, Connecticut, Mr. Hamilton from New York, New Jersey, Pennsylvania, Delaware, Maryland, Virginia, North Carolina, South Carolina, and Georgia;

RESOLVED
That the preceding Constitution be laid before the United States in Congress assembled, and that it is the opinion of this Convention, that it should afterwards be submitted to a convention of delegates, chosen in each State by the people thereof, under the recommendation of its legislature, for their assent and ratification; and that each convention assenting to, and ratifying the same, should give notice thereof to the United States in Congress assembled.

Resolved, that it is the opinion of this convention, that as soon as the conventions of nine States shall have ratified this Constitution, the United States in Congress assembled should fix a day on which electors should be appointed by the States which shall have ratified the same, and a day on which the electors should assemble to vote for the President, and the time and place for commencing proceedings under this Constitution. That after such publication the electors should be appointed, and the senators and Representatives elected: That the electors should meet on the day fixed for the election of the President, and should transmit their votes certified, signed, sealed and directed, as the Constitution requires, to the Secretary of the United States in

Congress assembled, that the Senators and Representatives should convene at the time and place assigned; that the Senators should appoint a President of the Senate, for the sole purpose of receiving, opening, and counting the votes for President; and, that after he shall be chosen, the Congress, together with the President, should, without delay, proceed to execute this Constitution.

By the unanimous order of the Convention.

George Washington, President.
William Jackson, Secretary.

The BILL OF RIGHTS
As provided in the FIRST TEN
AMENDMENTS
TO THE CONSTITUTION OF THE
UNITED STATES
Effective December 15, 1791

Articles in addition to, and amendment of the Constitution of the United States of America, proposed by Congress, and ratified by the legislatures of the several States, pursuant to the fifth article of the original Constitution.

PREAMBLE
The conventions of a number of the States having at the time of their adopting the Constitution, expressed a desire, in order to prevent misconstruction or abuse of its powers, that further declaratory and restrictive clauses should be added: And, as extending the ground of public confidence in the government, will best insure the beneficent ends of its institution.

[Articles I through X, now known as the Bill of Rights, were proposed on September 25, 1789; and declared in force on December 15, 1791.]

Article I
Congress shall make no law respecting an establishment of religion, or prohibiting the free exercise thereof; or abridging the freedom of speech, or of the press; or the right of the people peaceably to assemble, and to petition the government for a redress of grievances.

Article II
A well regulated militia, being necessary to the security of a free State, the right of the people to keep and bear arms, shall not be infringed.

Article III
No soldier shall, in time of peace be quartered in any house,

without the consent of the owner, nor in time of war, but in a manner to be prescribed by law.

Article IV

The right of the people to be secure in their person, houses, papers, and effects, against unreasonable searches and seizures, shall not be violated, and no warrants shall issue, but upon probable cause, supported by oath or affirmation, and particularly describing the place to be searched, and the persons or things to be seized.

Article V

No person shall be held to answer for a capital, or otherwise infamous crime, unless on a presentment or indictment of a Grand Jury, except in cases arising in the land or naval forces, or in the militia, when in actual service in time of war or public danger; nor shall any person be subject for the same offence to be twice put in jeopardy of life or limb; nor shall be compelled in any criminal case to be a witness against himself, nor be deprived of life, liberty, or property, without due process of law; nor shall private property be taken for public use, without just compensation.

Article VI

In all criminal prosecutions, the accused shall enjoy the right to a speedy and public trial, by an impartial jury of the State and district wherein the crime shall have been committed, which district shall have been previously ascertained by law, and to be informed of the nature and cause of the accusation; to be confronted with the witnesses against him; to have compulsory process for obtaining witnesses in his favor, and to have the assistance of counsel for his defence.

Article VII

In suits at common law, where the value in controversy shall exceed twenty dollars, the right of trial by jury shall be preserved, and no fact tried by a jury shall be otherwise re-examined in any court of the United States, than according to the rules of the common law.

Article VIII

Excessive bail shall not be required, nor excessive fines imposed, nor cruel and unusual punishments inflicted.

Article IX

The enumeration in the Constitution, of certain rights, shall not be construed to deny or disparage others retained by the people.

Article X

The powers not delegated to the United States by the Constitution, nor prohibited by it to the States, are reserved to the States respectively, or to the people.

Article XI

[Proposed March 4, 1794; declared ratified January 8, 1798]

The judicial power of the United States shall not be construed to extend to any suit in law or equity, commenced or prosecuted against one of the United States by citizens of another State, or by citizens or subjects of any foreign State.

Article XII

[Proposed December 9, 1803; declared ratified September 25, 1804]

The electors shall meet in their respective States, and vote by ballot for President and Vice-President, one of whom, at least, shall not be an inhabitant of the same State with themselves; they shall name in their ballots the person voted for as President, and in distinct ballots the person voted for as Vice-President, and of the number of votes for each, which lists they shall sign and certify, and transmit sealed to the seat of the government of the United States, directed to the President of the Senate;—The President of the Senate shall, in the presence of the Senate and House of Representatives, open all the certificates and the votes shall then be counted;—The person having the greatest number of votes for President, shall be the President, if such number be a majority of the whole number of electors appointed; and if no person have such majority, then from the persons having the highest numbers not exceeding three on the list of those voted for as President, the House of Representatives shall choose immediately, by ballot, the President. But in choosing the President, the votes shall be taken by States, the representation from each State having one vote; a quorum for this purpose shall consist of a member or members from two-thirds of the states, and a majority of all the states shall be necessary to a choice. And if the House of Representatives shall not choose a President whenever the right of choice shall devolve upon them, before the fourth day of March next following, then the Vice-President shall devolve upon them, before the fourth day of March next following, then the Vice-President shall act as President, as in the case of death or other constitutional disability of the President. The person having the greatest number of votes as Vice-President, shall be the Vice-President, if such number be a majority of the whole number of electors appointed, and if no person have a majority, then from the two highest numbers on the list, the Senate shall choose the Vice-President; a quorum for the purpose shall consist of two-thirds of the whole number of Senators, and a majority of the whole number shall be necessary to a choice. But no person consitutionally ineligible to the office of President shall be eligible to that of Vice-President of the United States.

Article XIII
[Proposed January 31, 1865; declared ratified December 18, 1865]
Section 1. Neither slavery nor involuntary servitude, except as a punishment for crime whereof the party shall have been duly convicted, shall exist within the United States or any place subject to their jurisdiction.

Section 2. Congress shall have power to enforce this article by appropriate legislation.

Article XIV
[Proposed June 13, 1866; declared ratified July 28, 1868]
Section 1. All persons born or naturalized in the United States, and subject to the jurisdiction thereof, are citizens of the United States and of the State wherein they reside. No State shall make or enforce any law which shall abridge the privileges or immunities of citizens of the United States; Nor shall any State deprive any person of life, liberty, or property, without due process of law; nor deny to any person within its jurisdiction the equal protection of the laws.

Section 2. Representatives shall be apportioned among the several States according to their respective numbers, counting the whole number of persons in each State, excluding Indians not taxed. But when the right to vote at any election for the choice of electors for President and Vice-President of the United States, Representatives in Congress, the executive and judicial officers of a State, or the members of the legislature thereof, is denied to any of the male inhabitants of such State, being twenty-one years of age, and citizens of the United States, or in any way abridged, except for participation in rebellion, or other crime, the basis of representation therein shall be reduced in the proportion which the number of such male citizens shall bear to the whole number of male citizens twenty-one years of age in such State.

Section 3. No person shall be a Senator or Representative in Congress, or elector of President and Vice-President, or hold any office, civil or military, under the United States, or under any State, who, having previously taken an oath, as a member of Congress, or as an officer of the United States, or as a member of any State legislature, or as an executive or judicial officer of any State, to support the Constitution of the United States, shall have engaged in insurrection or rebellion against the same, or given aid or comfort to the enemies thereof. But Congress may by a vote of two-thirds of each House, remove such disability.

Section 4. The validity of the public debt of the United States, authorized by law, including debts incurred for payment of pensions and bounties for services in suppressing insurrection or rebellion, shall not be questioned. But neither the United States, nor any State shall assume or pay any debt or obligation incurred in aid of insurrection or rebellion against the United States, or any claim for the loss or emancipation of any slave, but all such debts, obligations and claims shall be held illegal and void.

Article XV
[Proposed February 25, 1869; declared ratified March 30, 1870]
Section 1. The right of citizens of the United States to vote shall not be denied or abridged by the United States or by any State on account of race, color, or previous condition of servitude.

Section 2. The Congress shall have power to enforce this article by appropriate legislation.

Article XVI
[Proposed July 12, 1909; declared ratified February 25, 1913]
The Congress shall have power to lay and collect taxes on incomes, from whatever source derived, without apportionment among the several States, and without regard to any census or enumeration.

Article XVII
[Proposed May 13, 1912; declared ratified May 31, 1913]
The Senate of the United States shall be composed of two Senators from each State, elected by the people thereof, for six years; and each Senator shall have one vote. The electors in each State shall have the qualifications requisite for electors of the most numerous branch of the State legislatures.

When vacancies happen in the representation of any State in the Senate, the executive authority of such State shall issue writs of election to fill such vacancies: *Provided,* That the legislature of any State may empower the executive thereof to make temporary appointments until the people fill the vacancies by election as the legislature may direct.

This amendment shall not be so contrued as to affect the election or term of any Senator chosen before it becomes valid as part of the Constitution.

Article XVIII
[Proposed December 18, 1917; declared ratified January 29, 1919]
[Repealed by the Twenty-first Amendment December 5, 1933]

Section 1. After one year from the ratification of this article the manufacture, sale, or transportation of intoxicating liquors within, the importation thereof into, or the exportation thereof from the United States and all territory subject to the jurisdiction thereof for beverage purposes is hereby prohibited.

Section 2. The Congress and the several States shall have concurrent power to enforce this article by appropriate legislation.

Section 3. This article shall be inoperative unless it shall have been ratified as an amendment to the Constitution by the legislatures of the several States, as provided in the Constitution, within seven years from the date of submission hereof to the States by the Congress.

Article XIX
[Proposed June 4, 1919; declared ratified August 26, 1920]

The right of citizens of the United States to vote shall not be denied or abridged by the United States or by any State on account of sex.

Congress shall have power to enforce this article by appropriate legislation.

Article XX
[Proposed March 2, 1932; declared ratified February 6, 1933]

Section 1. The terms of the President and Vice-President shall end at noon on the 20th day of January, and the terms of Senators and Representatives at noon on the 3rd day of January, of the year in which such terms would have ended if this article had not been ratified; and the terms of their successors shall then begin.

Section 2. The Congress shall assemble at least once in every year, and such meeting shall begin at noon on the 3rd day of January, unless they shall by law appoint a different day.

Section 3. If, at the time fixed for the beginning of the term of the President, the President elect shall have died, the Vice President elect shall become President. If a President shall not have been chosen before the time fixed for the beginning of his term, or if the President elect shall have failed to qualify, then the Vice President elect shall act as President until a President shall have qualified; and the Congress may by law provide for the case wherein neither a President elect nor a Vice President elect shall have qualified, declaring who shall then act as President, or the manner in which one who is to act shall be selected, and such person shall act accordingly until a President or Vice President shall have qualified.

Section 4. The Congress may by law provide for the case of the death of any of the persons from whom the House of Representatives may choose a President whenever the right of choice shall have devolved upon them, and for the case of the death of any of the persons from whom the Senate may choose a Vice President whenever the right of choice shall have devolved upon them.

Section 5. Sections 1 and 2 shall take effect on the 15th day of October following the ratification of this article.

Section 6. This article shall be inoperative unless it shall have been ratified as an amendment to the Constitution by the legislatures of three-fourths of the several States within seven years from the date of its submission.

Article XXI
[Proposed February 20, 1933; declared ratified December 5, 1933]

Section 1. The eighteenth article of amendment to the Constitution of the United States is hereby repealed.

Section 2. The transportation or importation into any State, Territory, or possession of the United States for delivery or use therein of intoxicating liquors, in violation of the laws thereof, is hereby prohibited.

Section 3. This article shall be inoperative unless it shall have been ratified as an amendment to the Constitution by conventions in the several States, as provided in the Constitution, within seven years from the date of the submission hereof to the States by the Congress.

Article XXII
[Proposed March 24, 1947; declared ratified March 1, 1951]

Section 1. No person shall be elected to the office of President more than twice, and no person who has held the office of President, or acted as President, for more than two years of a term to which some other person was elected President shall be elected to the office of the President more than once. But this article shall not apply to any person holding the office of President when this article was proposed by the Congress, and shall not prevent any person who may be holding the office of President, or acting as President, during the term within which this article becomes operative from holding the office of President or acting as President during the remainder of such term.

Section 2. This article shall be inoperative unless it shall have been ratified as an amendment to the Constitution by the legislatures of three-fourths of the several States within seven years from the date of its submission to the States by the Congress.

Article XXIII
[Proposed June 16, 1960; declared ratified April 3, 1961]

Section 1. The District constituting the seat of government of the United States shall appoint in such manner as the Congress may direct:

A number of electors of President and Vice President equal to the whole number of Senators and Representatives in Congress to which the District would be entitled if it were a State, but in no event more than the least populous State; they shall be in addition to those appointed by the States, but they shall be considered, for the purposes of the election of President and Vice President to be electors appointed by a State; and they shall meet in the District and perform such duties as provided by the twelfth article of amendment.

Section 2. The Congress shall have power to enforce this article by appropriate legislation.

Article XXIV
[Proposed August 27, 1962; declared ratified February 4, 1964]

Section 1. The right of citizens of the United States to vote in any primary or other election for President or Vice President, for electors for President or Vice President, or for Senator or Representative in Congress, shall not be denied or abridged by the United States or any State by reason of failure to pay any poll tax or other tax.

Section 2. The Congress shall have power to enforce this article by appropriate legislation.

Article XXV
[Proposed July 6, 1965; declared ratified February 23, 1967]

Section 1. In case of the removal of the President from office or of his death or resignation, the Vice President shall become President.

Section 2. Whenever there is a vacancy in the office of the Vice President, the President shall nominate a Vice President who shall take the office upon confirmation by a majority vote of both Houses of Congress.

Section 3. Whenever the President transmits to the President pro tempore of the Senate and the Speaker of the House of Representatives his written declaration that he is unable to discharge the powers and duties of his office, and until he transmits to them a written declaration to the contrary, such powers and duties shall be discharged by the Vice President as Acting President.

Section 4. Whenever the Vice President and a majority of either the principal officers of the executive departments or of such other body as

Congress may by law provide, transmit to the President pro tempore of the Senate and The Speaker of the House of Representatives their written declaration that the President is unable to discharge the powers and duties of his office, the Vice President shall immediately assume the powers and duties of the office as Acting President.

Thereafter, when the President transmits to the President pro tempore of the Senate and the Speaker of the House of Representatives his written declaration that no inability exists, he shall resume the powers and duties of his office unless the Vice President and a majority of either the principal officers of the executive department or of such other body as Congress may by law provide, transmit within four days to the President pro tempore of the Senate and The Speaker of the House of Representative their written declaration that the President is unable to discharge the powers and duties of his office. Thereupon Congress shall decide the issue, assembling within 48 hours for that purpose if not in session. If the Congress is not in session, within 21 days after Congress is required to assemble, determines by two-thirds vote of both houses that the President is unable to discharge the powers and duties of his office, the Vice President shall continue to discharge the same as Acting President; otherwise, the President shall resume the powers and duties of his office.

Article XXVI
[Proposed March 23, 1971; declared ratified July 5, 1971]

Section 1. The right of citizens of the United States, who are eighteen years of age or older, to vote shall not be denied or abridged by the United States or by any State on account of age.

Section 2. The Congress shall have power to enforce this article by appropriate legislation.

Proposed Equal Rights Amendment
[Proposed March 22, 1972; declared ratified—]

Section 1. Equality of rights under the law shall not be denied or abridged by the United States or by any State on account of sex.

Section 2. The Congress shall have the power to enforce, by appropriate legislation, the provisions of this article.

Section 3. This Amendment shall take effect two years after the date of ratification. (Proposed March 22, 1972 - Not yet ratified.)

THE GREAT
SNOW JOB

PART IV

THE COURT
SPEAKS

Cite: 36 S Ct 236 (1916)

(240 U. S. 1)
FRANK R. BRUSHABER, Appt.,
v.
UNION PACIFIC RAILROAD COMPANY.

INTERNAL REVENUE #28—INJUNCTION AGAINST TAX—
STOCKHOLDER'S SUIT.

1. The maintenance by a stockholder of a suit to restrain a corporation from voluntarily complying with the income tax provisions of the
tariff act of October 3, 1913 (38 Stat. at L. 166, chap. 16), upon the
grounds of the repugnancy of the statute to the Federal Constitution, of
the peculiar relation of the corporation to the stockholders, and their
particular interests resulting from many of the administrative provisions
of the assailed act, of the confusion, wrong, and multiplicity of suits,
and the absence of all means of redress, which will result if the corporation pays the tax and complies with the act in other respects without
protest, as it is alleged it is its intention to do, is not forbidden by the
prohibition of U. S. Rev. Stat. § 3224, Comp. Stat. 1913, § 5947, against
enjoining the enforcement of taxes.

[Ed. Note.—For other cases, see Internal Revenue, Cent. Dig. §§ 76-
81; Dec. Dig. #28.]

INTERNAL REVENUE #7—POWER OF CONGRESS—INCOME TAX.

2. The whole purpose of U. S. Const., 16th Amend., giving Congress the power "to lay and collect taxes on incomes, from whatever
source derived, without apportionment among the several states, and
without regard to any census or enumeration," was to exclude the
source from which a taxed income was derived as the criterion by
which to determine the applicability of the constitutional requirement
as to apportionment of direct taxes.

[Ed. Note.—For other cases, see Internal Revenue, Cent. Dig. §§ 8-
10; Dec. Dig. #7.]

CONSTITUTIONAL LAW #286—INTERNAL REVENUE #2—DUE
PROCESS OF LAW—INCOME TAX—RETROACTIVE EFFECT.

3. The retroactive effect of the income tax provisions of the tariff
act of October 3, 1913 (38 Stat. at L. 166, chap. 16), which fix the

---

(#) = West Key number system. For other cases see same topic & KEY-
NUMBER in all Key-Numbered Digests & Indexes.

preceding March 1st as the time from which the taxed income for the first ten months is to be computed, does not render the tax repugnant to the due process of law clause of U. S. Const., 5th Amend., nor inconsistent with the 16th Amendment itself, since the date of retroactivity did not extend beyond the time when the latter Amendment became operative.

[Ed. Note.—For other cases, see Constitutional Law, Dec. Dig. #286: Internal Revenue, Cent. Dig. § 2; Dec. Dig. #2.]

INTERNAL REVENUE #2—INCOME TAX—EXEMPTIONS.

4. Power to exclude from taxation some income of designated persons and classes, and to exempt entirely certain enumerated organizations or corporations, such as labor, agricultural, or horticultural organizations, mutual savings banks, etc., was not by implication forbidden to Congress by the provisions of U. S. Const., 16th Amend., that Congress may lay and collect taxes on incomes "from whatever source derived."

[Ed. Note.—For other cases, see Internal Revenue, Cent. Dig. § 2; Dec. Dig. #2.]

INTERNAL REVENUE #2—INCOME TAX—EXEMPTIONS.

5. Labor, agricultural, or horticultural organizations, mutual savings banks, etc., could be excepted from the operation of the income tax provisions of the tariff act of October 3, 1913 (38 Stat. at L. 166, chap. 16), without rendering the tax repugnant to the Federal Constitution.

[Ed. Note.—For other cases, see Internal Revenue, Cent. Dig. § 2; Dec. Dig. #2.]

TAXATION #40—INTERNAL REVENUE—INCOME TAX—UNIFORMITY.

6. A geographical uniformity alone is what is exacted by the provisions of U. S. Const., art. 1, § 8, that "all duties, imposts, and excises shall be uniform throughout the United States."

[Ed. Note.—For other cases, see Taxation, Cent. Dig. §§ 68-89; Dec. Dig. #40.]

CONSTITUTIONAL LAW #283 — DUE PROCESS OF LAW—INCOME TAX.

7. The due process of law clause of U.S. Const., 5th Amend., is not a limitation upon the taxing power conferred upon Congress by the Federal Constitution unless, under a seeming exercise of the taxing power, the taxing statute is so arbitrary as to compel the conclusion that

it was not the exertion of taxation, but the confiscation of property, or is so wanting in basis for classification as to produce such a gross and patent inequality as inevitably to lead to the same conclusion.

[Ed. Note.—For other cases, see Constitutional Law, Cent. Dig. §§ 891, 892, 904-906; Dec. Dig. #283.]

CONSTITUTIONAL LAW #286 —DUE PROCESS OF LAW—INCOME TAX.

8. The progressive rate feature of the income tax imposed by the act of October 3, 1913 (38 Stat. at L. 166, chap. 16), does not cause such tax to transcend the conception of all taxation, and to be a mere arbitrary abuse of power which must be treated as wanting in due process of law.

[Ed. Note.—For other cases, see Constitutional Law, Dec. Dig. #286.]

CONSTITUTIONAL LAW #286 —DUE PROCESS OF LAW—INCOME TAX—DISCRIMINATION

9. The methods of collection at the source, prescribed by the income tax provisions of the tariff act of October 3, 1913 (38 Stat. at L. 166, chap. 16), are not wanting in due process of law because of the cost to which corporations are subjected by the duty of collection cast upon them, nor because of the resulting discrimination between corporations indebted upon coupon and registered bonds and those not so indebted, nor because of the discrimination against corporations which have assumed the payment of taxes on their bonds which results from the fact that some or all of their bondholders may be exempt from the income tax, nor because of the discrimination against owners of corporate bonds in favor of individuals none of whose income is derived from such property, nor because the law does not release corporate bondholders from the payment of a tax on their bonds, even after such taxes have been deducted by the corporation, if, after the deduction, the corporation should fail, nor because the payment of the tax by the corporation does not relieve the owners of bonds, the taxes on which have been assumed by the corporation, from their duty to include the income from such bonds in making a return of all income.

[Ed. Note.—For other cases, see Constitutional Law, Dec. Dig. #286.]

CONSTITUTIONAL LAW #286 —DUE PROCESS OF LAW—INCOME TAX—DISCRIMINATION.

10. Limiting the amount of interest which may be deducted from

gross income of a corporation for the purpose of fixing the taxable income to interest on indebtedness not exceeding one half the sum of bonded indebtedness and paid-up capital stock, as is done by the income tax provisions of the tariff act of October 3, 1913 (38 Stat. at L. 166, chap. 16), is not wanting in due process of law because discriminating between different classes of corporations and individuals.

[Ed. Note.—For other cases, see Constitutional Law, Dec. Dig. #286.]

CONSTITUTIONAL LAW #286 —DUE PROCESS OF LAW—INCOME TAX—DISCRIMINATION.

11. Allowing individuals to deduct from their gross income dividends paid them by corporations whose incomes are taxed, and not giving such right of deduction to corporations, as is done by the income tax provisions of the tariff act of October 3, 1913 (38 Stat. at L. 166, chap. 16), does not render the tax wanting in due process of law.

[Ed. Note.—For other cases, see Constitutional Law, Dec. Dig. #286.]

CONSTITUTIONAL LAW #286 —DUE PROCESS OF LAW—INCOME TAX—DISCRIMINATION.

12. The allowance of a deduction of $3,000 or $4,000 to those who pay the normal tax, as is done by the income tax provisions of the tariff act of October 3, 1913 (38 Stat. at L. 166, chap. 16), is not wanting in due process of law because those whose incomes are greater than $20,000 are not allowed, for the purpose of the additional or progressive tax, a second right to deduct the $3,000 or $4,000 which they have already enjoyed, nor because, for the purpose of the additional tax, no second right to deduct dividends received from corporations is permitted.

[Ed. Note.—For other cases, see Constitutional Law, Dec. Dig. #286.]

CONSTITUTIONAL LAW #286 —DUE PROCESS OF LAW—INCOME TAX—DISCRIMINATION.

13. The allowance of a deduction of stated amounts for the purpose of ascertaining the taxable income, as is done by the income tax provisions of the tariff act of October 3, 1913 (38 Stat. at L. 166, chap. 16), does not render the tax wanting in due process of law because of the discrimination between married and single people, and between husbands and wives who are living together and those who are not.

[Ed. Note.—For other cases, see Constitutional Law, Dec. Dig.

130

#286.]

CONSTITUTIONAL LAW #206, 286 —DUE PROCESS OF LAW—
INCOME TAX—DISCRIMINATION.

14. No unconstitutional discrimination and want of due process of law results because the owners of houses in which they live are not compelled by the income tax provisions of the tariff act of October 3, 1913 (38 Stat. at L. 166, chap. 16), to estimate the rental value in making up their incomes, while those who live in rented houses are not allowed, in making up their taxable income, to deduct the rent which they have paid, nor because of the fact that although family expenses are not, as a rule, permitted to be deducted from gross income, farmers are permitted to omit from their income return certain products of the farm which are susceptible of use by them for sustaining their families during the year.

[Ed. Note.—For other cases, see Constitutional Law, Cent. Dig. §§ 625-648; Dec. Dig. #206, 286.]

CONSTITUTIONAL LAW #62—DELEGATION OF POWER—ADMINISTRATION OF INCOME TAX

15. An unwarrantable delegation of legislative authority was not made by the income tax provisions of the tariff act of October 3, 1913 (38 Stat. at L. 166, chap. 16), because certain administrative powers to enforce the act were conferred by it upon the Secretary of the Treasury.

[Ed. Note.—For other cases, see Constitutional Law, Cent. Dig. §§ 94-102; Dec. Dig. #62.]

[No. 140.]

Argued October 14 and 15, 1915. Decided January 24, 1916.

APPEAL from the District Court of the United States for the Southern District of New York to review a decree dismissing the bill in a suit by a stockholder to restrain the corporation from voluntarily complying with the Federal income tax. Affirmed.

The facts are stated in the opinion.

Messrs. **Julien T. Davies**, Brainard Tolles, Garrard Glenn, and Martin A. Schenck for appellant.

Mr. Henry W. Clark for appellee.

Solicitor General **Davis**, Assistant Attorney General **Wallace**, and Attorney General Gregory for the United States.

Mr. Chief Justice **White** delivered the opinion of the court:

As a stockholder of the Union Pacific Railroad Company, the appellant filed his bill to enjoin the corporation from complying with the income tax provisions of the tariff act of October 3, 1913 (§ II., chap. 16, 38 Stat. at L. 166). Because of constitutional questions duly arising the case is here on direct appeal from a decree sustaining a motion to dismiss because no ground for relief was stated.

The right to prevent the corporation from returning and paying the tax was based upon many averments as to the repugnancy of the statute to the Constitution of the United States, of the peculiar relation of the corporation to the stockholders, and their particular interests resulting from many of the administrative provisions of the assailed act, of the confusion, wrong, and multiplicity of suits and the absence of all means of redress which would result if the corporation paid the tax and complied with the act in other respects without protest, as it was alleged it was its intention to do. To put out of the way a question of jurisdiction we at once say that in view of these averments and the ruling in Pollock v. Farmers' Loan & T. Co. 157 U. S. 429, 39 L. ed. 759, 15 Sup. Ct. Rep. 673, sustaining the right of a stockholder to sue to restrain a corporation under proper averments from voluntarily paying a tax charged to be unconstitutional on the ground that to permit such a suit did not violate the prohibitions of § 3224, Revised Statutes (Comp. Stat. 1913, § 5947), against enjoining the enforcement of taxes, we are of opinion that the contention here made that there was no jurisdiction of the cause, since to entertain it would violate the provisions of the Revised Statutes referred to, is without merit. Before coming to dispose of the case on the merits, however, we observe that the defendant corporation having called the attention of the government to the pendency of the cause and the nature of the controversy and its unwillingness to voluntarily refuse to comply with the act assailed, the United States, as amicus curiae, has at bar been heard both orally and by brief for the purpose of sustaining the decree.

Aside from averments as to citizenship and residence, recitals as to the provisions of the statute, and statements as to the business of the corporation, contained in the first ten paragraphs of the bill, advanced to sustain jurisdiction, the bill alleged twenty-one constitutional objections specified in that number of paragraphs or subdivisions. As all the grounds assert a violation of the Constitution, it follows that, in a wide sense, they all charge a repugnancy of the statute to the 16th Amendment, under the more immediate sanction of which the statute was adopted.

The various propositions are so intermingled as to cause it to be difficult to classify them. We are of opinion, however, that the confusion is not inherent, but rather arises from the conclusion that the 16th Amendment provides for a hitherto unknown power of taxation; that is, a power to levy an income tax which, although direct, should not be subject to the regulation of apportionment applicable to all other direct taxes. And the far-reaching effect of this erroneous assumption will be made clear by generalizing the many contentions advanced in argument to support it, as follows: (a) The Amendment authorizes only a particular character of direct tax without apportionment, and therefore if a tax is levied under its assumed authority which does not partake of the characteristics exacted by the Amendment, it is outside of the Amendment, and is void as a direct tax in the general constitutional sense because not apportioned. (b) As the Amendment authorizes a tax only upon incomes "from whatever source derived," the exclusion from taxation of some income of designated persons and classes is not authorized, and hence the constitutionality of the law must be tested by the general provisions of the Constitution as to taxation, and thus again the tax is void for want of apportionment. (c) As the right to tax "incomes from whatever source derived" for which the Amendment provides must be considered as exacting intrinsic uniformity, therefore no tax comes under the authority of the Amendment not conforming to such standard, and hence all the provisions of the assailed statute must once more be tested solely under the general and pre-existing provisions of the Constitution, causing the statute again to be void in the absence of apportionment. (d) As the power conferred by the Amendment is new and prospective, the attempt in the statute to make its provisions retroactively apply is void because, so far as the retroactive period is concerned, it is governed by the pre-existing constitutional requirement as to apportionment.

But it clearly results that the proposition and the contentions under it, if acceded to, would cause one provision of the Constitution to destroy another; that is, they would result in bringing the provisions of the Amendment exempting a direct tax from apportionment into irreconcilable conflict with the general requirement that all direct taxes be apportioned. Moreover, the tax authorized by the Amendment, being direct, would not come under the rule of uniformity applicable under the Constitution to other than direct taxes, and thus it would come to pass that the result of the Amendment would be to authorize a particular direct tax not subject either to apportionment or to the rule of geographical uniformity, thus giving power to impose a different tax in one state or states than was levied in another state or states. This result, instead of simplifying the situation and making clear the limitations on the taxing power, which obviously the Amendment must have been intended to accomplish, would create radical and destructive changes in our constitutional system and multiply confusion.

But let us by a demonstration of the error of the fundamental proposition as to the significance of the Amendment dispel the confusion necessarily arising from the arguments deduced from it. Before coming, however, to the text of the Amendment, to the end that its significance may be determined in the light of the previous legislative and judicial history of the subject with which the Amendment is concerned, and with a knowledge of the conditions which presumptively led up to its adoption, and hence of the purpose it was intended to accomplish, we make a brief statement on those subjects.

That the authority conferred upon Congress by § 8 of article 1 "to lay and collect taxes, duties, imposts and excises" is exhaustive and embraces every conceivable power of taxation has never been questioned, or, if it has, has been so often authoritatively declared as to render it necessary only to state the doctrine. And it has also never been questioned from the foundation, without stopping presently to determine under which of the separate headings the power was properly to be classed, that there was authority given, as the part was included in the whole, to lay and collect income taxes. Again, it has never moreover been questioned that the conceded complete and all-embracing taxing power was subject, so far as they were respectively applicable, to limitations resulting from the requirements of art. 1, § 8, cl. 1, that "all duties, imposts and excises shall be uniform throughout the United States," and to the limitations of art. 1, § 2, cl. 3, that "direct taxes shall be apportioned among the several states," and of art. 1, § 9, cl. 4, that "no capitation, or other direct tax shall be laid, unless in proportion to the census or enumeration hereinbefore directed to be taken." In fact, the two great subdivisions embracing the complete and perfect delegation of the power to tax and the two correlated limitations as to such power were thus aptly stated by Mr. Chief Justice Fuller in Pollock v. Farmers' Loan & T. Co. 157 U. S. supra, at page 557: "In the matter of taxation, the Constitution recognizes the two great classes of direct and indirect taxes, and lays down two rules by which their imposition must be governed, namely: The rule of apportionment as to direct taxes, and the rule of uniformity as to duties, imposts, and excises." It is to be observed, however, as long ago pointed out in Veazie Bank v. Fenno, 8 Wall. 533, 541, 19 L. ed. 482, 485, that the requirements of apportionment as to one of the great classes and of uniformity as to the other class were not so much a limitation upon the complete and all-embracing authority to tax, but in their essence were simply regulations concerning the mode in which the plenary power was to be exerted. In the whole history of the government down to the time of the adoption of the 16th Amendment, leaving aside some conjectures expressed of the possibility of a tax lying intermediate between the two great classes and embraced by neither, no question has been anywhere made as to the correctness of these propositions. At the very beginning, however, there arose differences of opinion concerning the criteria to be applied in determining in which of the two great subdivisions a tax would fall. Without pausing to state at length the basis of these differences and the consequences which arose from them, as the whole subject was elaborately reviewed in Pollock v. Farmers' Loan & T. Co. 157 U. S. 429, 39 L. ed. 759, 15 Sup. Ct. Rep. 673, 158 U. S. 601, 39 L. ed. 1108, 15 Sup. Ct. Rep. 912, we make a condensed statement which is in substance taken from what was said in that case. Early the differences were manifested in pressing on the one hand and opposing on the other, the passage of an act levying a tax without apportionment on carriages "for the conveyance of persons," and when such a tax was enacted the question of its repugnancy to the Constitution soon came to this court for determination. Hylton v. United States, 3 Dall. 171, 1 L. ed. 556. It was held that the tax came within the class of excises, duties, and imposts, and therefore did not require apportionment, and while this conclusion was agreed to by all the members of the court who took part in the decision of the case, there was not an exact coincidence in the reasoning by which the conclusion was sustained. Without stating the minor differences, it may be said with substantial accuracy that the divergent reasoning was this: On the one hand, that the tax was not in the class of direct taxes requiring apportionment, because it was not levied directly on property because of its ownership, but rather on its use, and was therefore an excise, duty, or impost; and on the other, that in any event the class of direct taxes included only taxes directly levied on real estate because of its ownership. Putting out of view the difference of reasoning which led to the concurrent conclusion in the Hylton Case, it is undoubted that it came to pass in legislative practice that the line of demarcation between the two great classes of direct taxes on the one hand and excises, duties, and imposts on the other, which was exemplified by the ruling in that case, was accepted and acted upon. In the first place this is shown by the fact that wherever (and there were a number of cases of that kind) a tax was levied directly on real estate or slaves because of ownership, it was treated as coming within the direct class and apportionment was provided for, while no instance of apportionment as to any other kind of tax is afforded. Again the situation is aptly illustrated by the various acts taxing incomes derived from property of every kind and nature which were enacted beginning in 1861, and lasting during what may be termed the Civil War period. It is not disputable that these latter taxing laws were classed under the head of excises, duties, and imposts because it was assumed that they were of that character inasmuch as, although putting a tax burden on income of every kind, including that derived from property real or personal, they were not taxes directly on property because of its ownership. And this practical construction came in theory to be the accepted one, since it was adopted without dissent by the most eminent of the text writers. 1 Kent, Com. 254, 256; 1 Story, Const. § 955; Cooley, Const. Lim. 5th ed. *480; Miller, Constitution, 237; Pom. Const. Law, § 281; 1 Hare, Const. Law, 249, 250; Burroughs, Taxn. 502; Ordronaux, Constitutional Legislation, 225.

Upon the lapsing of a considerable period after the repeal of the income tax laws referred to, in 1894 [28 Stat. at L. 509, chap. 349], an act was passed laying a tax on incomes from all classes of property and other sources of revenue which was not apportioned, and which therefore was of course assumed to come within the classification of excises, duties, and imposts which were subject to the rule of uniformity, but not to the rule of apportionment. The constitutional validity of this law was challenged on the ground that it did not fall within the class of excises, duties, and imposts, but was direct in the constitutional sense, and was therefore void for want of apportionment, and that question came to this court and was passed upon in Pollock v. Farmers' Loan & T. Co. 157 U. S. 429, 39 L. ed. 759, 15 Sup. Ct. Rep. 673, 158 U. S. 601, 39 L. ed. 1108, 15 Sup. Ct. Rep. 912. The court, fully recognizing in the passage which we have previously quoted the all-embracing character of the two great classifications, including, on the one hand, direct taxes subject to apportionment, and on the other, excises, duties, and imposts subject to uniformity, held the law to be unconstitutional in substance for these reasons: Concluding that the classification of direct was adopted for the purpose of rendering it impossible to burden by taxation accumulations of property, real or personal, except subject to the regulation of apportionment, it was held that the duty existed to fix what was a direct tax in the constitutional sense so as to accomplish this purpose contemplated by the Constitution. (157 U. S. 581.) Coming to consider the validity of the tax from this point of view, while not questioning at all that in common understanding it was direct merely on income and only indirect on property, it was held that, considering the substance of things, it was direct on property in a constitutional sense, since to burden an income by a tax was, from the point of substance, to burden the property from which the income was derived, and thus accomplish the very thing which the provision as to apportionment of direct taxes was adopted to prevent. As this conclusion but enforced a regulation as to the mode of exercising power under particular circumstances, it did not in any way dispute the all-embracing taxing authority possessed by Congress, including necessarily therein the power to impose income taxes if only they conformed to the constitutional regulations which were applicable to them. Moreover, in addition, the conclusion reached in the Pollock Case did not in any degree involve holding that income taxes generically and necessarily came within the class of direct taxes on property, but, in the contrary, recognized the fact that taxation on income was in its nature an excise entitled to be enforced as such unless and until it was concluded that to enforce it would amount to accomplishing the result which the requirement as to apportionment of direct taxation was adopted to prevent, in which case the duty would arise to disregard form and consider substance alone, and hence subject the tax to the regulation as to apportionment which otherwise as an excise would not apply to it. Nothing could serve to make this clearer than to recall that in the Pollock Case, in so far as the law taxed incomes from other classes of property than real estate and invested personal property, that is, income from "professions, trades, employments, or vocations" (158 U. S. 637), its validity was recognized; indeed, it was expressly declared that no dispute was made upon that subject, and attention was called to the fact that taxes on such income had been sustained as excise taxes in the past. Id. p. 635. The whole law was, however, declared unconstitutional on the ground that to permit it to thus operate would relieve real estate and invested personal property from taxation and "would leave the burden of the tax to be borne by professions, trades, employments, or vocations; and in that way what was intended as a tax on capital would remain, in substance, a tax on occupations and labor" (id. p. 637),—a result which, it was held, could not have been contemplated by Congress.

This is the text of the Amendment:

"The Congress shall have power to lay and collect taxes on incomes, from whatever source derived, without apportionment among the several states, and without regard to any census or enumeration."

It is clear on the face of this text that it does not purport to confer power to levy income taxes in a generic sense,—an authority already possessed and never questioned,—or to limit and distinguish between one kind of income taxes and another, but that the whole purpose of the Amendment was to relieve all income taxes when imposed from apportionment from a consideration of the source whence the income was derived. Indeed, in the light of the history which we have given and of the decision in the Pollock Case, and the ground upon which the ruling in that case was based, there is no escape from the conclusion that the Amendment was drawn for the purpose of doing away for the future with the principle upon which the Pollock Case was decided; that is, of determining whether a tax on income was direct not by a consideration of the burden placed on the taxed income upon which it directly operated, but by taking into view the burden which resulted on the property from which the income was derived, since in express terms the Amendment provides that income taxes, from whatever source the income may be derived, shall not be subject to the regulation of apportionment. From this in substance it indisputably arises, first, that all the contentions which we have previously noticed concerning the assumed limitations to be implied from the language of the Amendment as to the nature and character of the income taxes which it authorizes find no support in the text and are in irreconcilable conflict with the very purpose which the Amendment was adopted to accomplish. Second, that the contention that the Amendment treats a tax on income as a direct tax although it is relieved from apportionment and is necessarily therefore not subject to the rule of uniformity as such rule only applies to taxes which are not direct, thus destroying the two great classifications which have been recognized and enforced from the beginning, is also wholly without foundation since the command of the Amendment that all income taxes shall not be subject to apportionment by a consideration of the sources from which the taxed income may be derived forbids the application to such taxes of the rule applied in the Pollock Case by which alone such taxes were removed from the great class of excises, duties, and imposts subject to the rule of uniformity, and were placed under the other or direct class. This must be unless it can be said that although the Constitution, as a result of the Amendment, in express terms excludes the criterion of source of income, that criterion yet remains for the purpose of destroying the classifications of the Constitution by taking an excise out of the class to which it belongs and transferring it to a class in which it cannot be placed consistently with the requirements of the Constitution. Indeed, from another point of view, the Amendment demonstrates that no such purpose was intended, and on the contrary shows that it was drawn with the object of maintaining the limitations of the Constitution and harmonizing their operation. We say this because it is to be observed that although from the date of the Hylton Case, because of statements made in the opinions in that case, it had come to be accepted that direct taxes in the constitutional sense were confined to taxes levied directly on real estate because of its ownership, the Amendment contains nothing repudiating or challenging the ruling in the Pollock Case that the word "direct" had a broader significance, since it embraced also taxes levied directly on personal property because of its ownership, and therefore the Amendment at least impliedly makes such wider significance a part of the Constitution,—a condition which clearly demonstrates that the purpose was not to change the existing interpretation except to the extent necessary to accomplish the result intended; that is, the prevention of the resort to the sources from which a taxed income was derived in order to cause a direct tax on the income to be a direct tax on the source itself, and thereby to take an income tax out of the class of excises, duties, and imposts, and place it in the class of direct taxes.

We come, then, to ascertain the merits of the many contentions made in the light of the Constitution as it now stands; that is to say, including within its terms the provisions of the 16th Amendment as correctly interpreted. We first dispose of two propositions assailing the validity of the statute on the one hand because of its repugnancy to the Constitution in other respects, and especially because its enactment was not authorized by the 16th Amendment.

The statute was enacted October 3, 1913, and provided for a general yearly income tax from December to December of each year. Exceptionally, however, it fixed a first period embracing only the time from March 1, to December 31, 1913, and this limited retroactivity is assailed as repugnant to the due process clause of the 5th Amendment, and as inconsistent with the 16th Amendment itself. But the date of the retroactivity did not extend beyond the time when the Amendment was operative, and there can be no dispute that there was power by virtue of the Amendment during that period to levy the tax, without apportionment, and so far as the limitations of the Constitution in other respects are concerned, the contention is not open, since in Stockdale v. Atlantic Ins. Co. 20 Wall. 323, 331, 22 L. ed. 348, 351, in sustaining a provision in a prior income tax law which was assailed because of its retroactive character, it was said:

"The right of Congress to have imposed this tax by a new statute, although the measure of it was governed by the income of the past year, cannot be doubted; much less can it be doubted that it could impose such a tax on the income of the current year, though part of that year had elapsed when the statute was passed. The joint resolution of July 4th, 1864 [13 Stat. at L. 417], imposed a tax of 5 per cent upon all income of the previous year, although one tax on it had already been paid, and no one doubted the validity of the tax or attempted to resist it."

The statute provides that the tax should not apply to enumerated organizations or corporations, such as labor, agricultural or horticultural organizations, mutual savings banks, etc., and the argument is that as the Amendment authorized a tax on incomes "from whatever source derived," by implication it excluded the power to make these exemptions. But this is only a form of expressing the erroneous contention as to the meaning of the Amendment, which we have already disposed of. And so far as this alleged illegality is based on other provisions of the Constitution, the contention is also not open, since it was expressly considered and disposed of in Flint v. Stone Tracy Co. 220 U. S. 108, 173, 55 L. ed. 389, 422, 31 Sup. Ct. Rep. 342, Ann. Cas. 1912B, 1312.

Without expressly stating all the other contentions, we summarize them to a degree adequate to enable us to typify and dispose of all of them.

1. The statute levies one tax called a normal tax on all incomes of individuals up to $20,000, and from that amount up, by gradations, a progressively increasing tax, called an additional tax, is imposed. No tax, however is levied upon incomes of unmarried individuals amounting to $3,000 or less, nor upon incomes of married persons amounting to $4,000 or less. The progressive tax and the exempted amounts, it is said, are based on wealth alone, and the tax is therefore repugnant to the due process clause of the 5th Amendment.

2. The act provides for collecting the tax at the source; that is, makes it the duty of corporations, etc., to retain and pay the sum of the tax on interest due on bonds and mortgages, unless the owner to whom the interest is payable gives a notice that he claims an exemption. This duty cast upon corporations, because of the cost to which they are subjected, is asserted to be repugnant to due process of law as a taking of their property without compensation, and we recapitulate various contentions as to discrimination against corporations and against individuals, predicated on provisions of the act dealing with the subject.

(a) Corporations indebted upon coupon and registered bonds are discriminated against, since corporations not so indebted are relieved of any labor or expense involved in deducting and paying the taxes of individuals on the income derived from bonds.

(b) Of the class of corporations indebted as above stated, the law further discriminates against those which have assumed the payment of taxes on their bonds, since although some or all of their bondholders may be exempt from taxation, the corporations have no means of ascertaining such fact, and it would therefore result that taxes would often be paid by such corporations when no taxes were owing by the individuals to the government.

(c) The law discriminates against owners of corporate bonds in favor of individuals none of whose income is derived from such property, since bondholders are, during the interval between the deducting and the paying of the tax on their bonds, deprived of the use of the money so withheld.

(d) Again, corporate bondholders are discriminated against because the law does not release them from payment of taxes on their bonds even after the taxes have been deducted by the corporation, and therefore if, after deduction, the corporation should fail, the bondholders would be compelled to pay the tax a second time.

(e) Owners of bonds the taxes on which have been assumed by the corporation are discriminated against because the payment of the taxes by the corporation does not relieve the bondholders of their duty to include the income from such bonds in making a return of all income, the result being a double payment of the taxes, labor and expense in applying for a refund, and a deprivation of the use of the sum of the taxes during the interval which elapses before they are refunded.

3. The provision limiting the amount of interest paid which may be deducted from gross income of corporations for the purpose of fixing the taxable income to interest on indebtedness not exceeding one half the sum of bonded indebtedness and paid-up capital stock is also charged to be wanting in due process because discriminating between different classes of corporations and individuals.

4. It is urged that want of due process results from the provision allowing individuals to deduct from their gross income dividends paid them by corporations whose incomes are taxed, and not giving such right of deduction to corporations.

5. Want of due process is also asserted to result from the fact that the act allows a deduction of $3,000 or $4,000 to those who pay the normal tax, that is, whose incomes are $20,000 or less, and does not allow the deduction to those whose incomes are greater than $20,000; that is, such persons are not allowed, for the purpose of the additional or progressive tax, a second right to deduct the $3,000 or $4,000 which they have already enjoyed. And a further violation of due process is based on the fact that for the purpose of the additional tax no second right to deduct dividends received from corporations is permitted.

6. In various forms of statement, want of due process, it is moreover insisted, arises from the provisions of the act allowing a deduction for the purpose of ascertaining the taxable income of stated amounts, on the ground that the provisions discriminate between married and single people, and discriminate between husbands and wives who are

living together and those who are not.

7. Discrimination and want of due process result, it is said, from the fact that the owners of houses in which they live are not compelled to estimate the rental value in making up their incomes, while those who are living in rented houses and pay rent are not allowed, in making up their taxable income, to deduct rent which they have paid, and that want of due process also results from the fact that although family expenses are not, as a rule, permitted to be deducted from gross, to arrive at taxable, income, farmers are permitted to omit from their income return certain products of the farm which are susceptible of use by them for sustaining their families during the year.

So far as these numerous and minute, not to say in many respects hypercritical, contentions are based upon an assumed violation of the uniformity clause, their want of legal merit is at once apparent, since it is settled that that clause exacts only a geographical uniformity, and there is not a semblance of ground in any of the propositions for assuming that a violation of such uniformity is complained of. Knowlton v. Moore, 178 U. S. 41, 44 L. ed. 969, 20 Sup. Ct. Rep. 747; Patton v. Brady, 184 U. S. 608, 622, 46 L. ed. 713, 720, 22 Sup. Ct. Rep. 493; Flint v. Stone Tracy Co. 220 U. S. 107, 158, 55 L. ed. 389, 416, 31 Sup. Ct. Rep. 342, Ann. Cas. 1912B, 1312; Billings v. United States, 232 U. S. 261, 282, 58 L. ed. 596, 605, 34 Sup. Ct. Rep. 421.

So far as the due process clause of the 5th Amendment is relied upon, it suffices to say that there is no basis for such reliance, since it is equally well settled that such clause is not a limitation upon the taxing power conferred upon Congress by the Constitution; in other words, that the Constitution does not conflict with itself by conferring, upon the one hand, a taxing power, and taking the same power away, on the other, by the limitations of the due process clause. Treat v. White, 181 U. S. 264, 45 L. ed. 853, 21 Sup. Ct. Rep. 611; Patton v. Brady, 184 U.S. 608, 46 L. ed. 713, 22 Sup. Ct. Rep. 493; McCray v. United States, 195 U.S. 27, 61, 49 L. ed. 78, 97, 24 Sup. Ct. Rep. 769, 1 Ann. Cas. 561; Flint v. Stone Tracy Co. 220 U. S. 107, 158, 55 L. ed. 389, 416, 31 Sup. Ct. Rep. 342, Ann. Cas. 1912B, 1312; Billings v. United States, 232 U. S. 261, 282, 58 L. ed. 596, 605, 34 Sup. Ct. Rep. 421. And no change in the situation here would arise even if it be conceded, as we think it must be, that this doctrine would have no application in a case where, although there was a seeming exercise of the taxing power, the act complained of was so arbitrary as to constrain to the conclusion that it was not the exertion of taxation, but a confiscation of property; that is, a taking of the same in violation of the 5th Amendment; or, what is equivalent thereto, was so wanting in basis for classification as to produce such a gross and patent inequality as to inevitably lead to the same conclusion. We say this because none of the propositions relied upon in the remotest degree present such questions. It is true that it is elaborately insisted that although there be no express constitutional provision prohibiting it, the progressive feature of the tax causes it to transcend the conception of all taxation and to be a mere arbitrary abuse of power which must be treated as wanting in due process. But the proposition disregards the fact that in the very early history of the government a progressive tax was imposed by Congress, and that such authority was exerted in some, if not all, of the various income taxes enacted prior to 1894 to which we have previously adverted. And over and above all this the contention but disregards the further fact that its absolute want of foundation in reason was plainly pointed out in Knowlton v. Moore, 178 U. S. 41, 44 L. ed. 969, 20 Sup. Ct. Rep. 747, and the right to urge it was necessarily foreclosed by the ruling in that case made. In this situation it is, of course, superfluous to say that arguments as to the expediency of levying such taxes, or of the economic mistake or wrong involved in their imposition, are beyond judicial cognizance. Besides this demonstration of the want of merit in the contention based upon the progressive feature of the tax, the error in the others is equally well established either by prior decisions or by the adequate bases for classification which are apparent on the face of the assailed provisions; that is, the distinction between individuals and corporations, the difference between various kinds of corporations, etc., etc. Ibid.; Flint v. Stone Tracy Co. 220 U. S. 107, 158, 55 L. ed. 389, 416, 31 Sup. Ct. Rep. 342, Ann. Cas. 1912B, 1312; Billings v. United States, 232 U. S. 261, 282, 58 L. ed. 596, 605, 34 Sup. Ct. Rep. 421; First Nat. Bank v. Kentucky, 9 Wall. 353, 19 L. ed. 701; National Safe Deposit Co. v. Stead, 232 U. S. 58, 70, 58 L. ed. 504, 510, 34 Sup. Ct. Rep. 209. In fact, comprehensively surveying all the contentions relied upon, aside from the erroneous construction of the Amendment which we have previously disposed of, we cannot escape the conclusion that they all rest upon the mistaken theory that although there be differences between the subjects taxed, to differently tax them transcends the limit of taxation and amounts to a want of due process, and that where a tax levied is believed by one who resists its enforcement to be wanting in wisdom and to operate injustice, from that fact in the nature of things there arises a want of due process of law and a resulting authority in the judiciary to exceed its powers and correct what is assumed to be mistaken or unwise exertions by the legislative authority of its lawful powers, even although there be no semblance of warrant in the Constitution for so doing.

We have not referred to a contention that because certain adminis-

143

trative powers to enforce the act were conferred by the statute upon the Secretary of the Treasury, therefore it was void as unwarrantedly delegating legislative authority, because we think to state the proposition is to answer it. Marshall Field & Co. v. Clark, 143 U. S. 649, 36 L. ed. 294, 12 Sup. Ct. Rep. 495; Buttfield v. Stranahan, 192 U. S. 470, 496, 48 L. ed. 525, 535, 24 Sup. Ct. Rep. 349; Oceanic Steam Nav. Co. v. Stranahan, 214 U. S. 320, 53 L. ed. 1013, 29 Sup. Ct. Rep. 671.

Affirmed.

Mr. Justice **McReynolds** took no part in the consideration and decision of this case.

Cite:111 S Ct 604 (1991)

John L. CHEEK, Petitioner,
v.
UNITED STATES.
No. 89-658.
Argued Oct. 3, 1990.
Decided Jan. 8, 1991.

Defendant was convicted in the United States District Court for the Northern District of Illinois, Paul E. Plunkett, J., of attempting to evade income taxes and failing to file income tax returns, and he appealed. The Court of Appeals for the Seventh Circuit affirmed, 822 F.2d 1263. The United States Supreme Court, Justice White, held that: (1) defendant was not entitled to acquittal based on good-faith belief that income tax law was unconstitutional as applied to him and thus did not legally impose any duty on him, but (2) defendant's good-faith belief that the tax laws did not impose any duty on him did not have to be objectively reasonable in order to be considered by the jury.

Vacated and remanded.

Justice Scalia, filed an opinion concurring in the judgement.

Justice Blackmun filed a dissenting opinion in which Justice Marshall joined.

Justice Souter did not participate.

1. Criminal Law #313
Based on the notion that the law is definite and knowable, common law presumed that every person knew the law.

2. Internal Revenue #5263.35
"Willfulness" for purposes of criminal tax laws requires the Government to prove that the law imposed a duty on the defendant, that the

---

defendant knew of the duty, and that he voluntarily and intentionally violated that duty. 26 U.S.C.A. §§ 7201, 7203.

See publication Words and Phrases for other judicial constructions and definitions.

3. Criminal Law #20

Where issue is whether defendant knew of duty purportedly imposed by statute or regulation he is accused of violating, if Government proves actual knowledge of the pertinent legal duty, the prosecution, without more, has satisfied the knowledge component of the willfulness requirement.

4. Internal Revenue #5300

Government has not proved that defendant was aware of the duty imposed by the tax law which he is accused of willfully disobeying if the jury credits a good-faith misunderstanding and belief submission, whether or not the claimed belief or misunderstanding is objectively reasonable. 26 U.S.C.A. §§ 7201, 7203.

5. Internal Revenue #5263.35

Defendant's claimed good-faith belief need not be objectively reasonable in order for it to negate Government's evidence purporting to show defendant's awareness of his duties under the tax laws. 26 U.S.C.A. §§ 7201, 7203.

6. Constitutional Law #38

Where possible, court interprets congressional enactments so as to avoid raising serious constitutional questions.

7. Internal Revenue #5317

It was error to instruct the jury to disregard evidence of defendant's understanding that, within meaning of the tax laws, he was not person required to file a return or to pay income taxes and that wages are not taxable income, as incredible as those misunderstandings of and beliefs about the tax law might be. 26 U.S.C.A. §§ 7201, 7203.

8. Internal Revenue #5263.35

Defendant's good-faith belief that income tax law was unconstitutional as applied to him did not provide defense to charges of willfully attempting to evade income taxes and failing to file income tax returns, notwithstanding claim that, because of his belief in the unconstitutionality of the tax laws as applied to him, the income tax laws could not legally impose any duty upon him of which he should have been aware. 26 U.S.C.A. §§ 7201, 7203.

Syllabus *

Petitioner Cheek was charged with six counts of willfully failing to file a federal income tax return in violation of § 7203 of the Internal Revenue Code (Code) and three counts of willfully attempting to evade his income taxes in violation of § 7201. Although admitting that he had not filed his returns, he testified that he had not acted willfully because he sincerely believed, based on his indoctrination by a group believing that the federal tax system is unconstitutional and his own study, that the tax laws were being unconstitutionally enforced and that his actions were lawful. In instructing the jury, the court stated that an honest but unreasonable belief is not a defense and does not negate willfulness, and that Cheek's beliefs that wages are not income and that he was not a taxpayer within the meaning of the Code were not objectively reasonable. It also instructed the jury that a person's opinion that the tax laws violate his constitutional rights does not constitute a good-faith misunderstanding of the law. Cheek was convicted, and the Court of Appeals affirmed.

Held:

1. A good-faith misunderstanding of the law or a good-faith belief that one is not violating the law negates willfulness, whether or not the claimed belief or misunderstanding is objectively reasonable. Statutory willfulness, which protects the average citizen from prosecution for innocent mistakes made due to the complexity of the tax laws, *United States v. Murdock,* 290 U.S. 389, 54 S.Ct. 223, 78 L.Ed. 381, is the voluntary, intentional violation of a known legal duty. *United States v. Pomponio,* 429 U.S. 10, 97 S.Ct. 22, 50 L.Ed.2d 12. Thus, if the jury credited Cheek's assertion that he truly believed that the Code did not treat wages as income, the Government would not have carried its burden to prove willfulness, however unreasonable a court might deem such a belief. Characterizing a belief as objectively unreasonable transforms what is normally a factual inquiry into a legal one, thus preventing a jury from considering it. And forbidding a jury to consider evidence that might negate willfulness would raise a serious question under the Sixth Amendment's jury trial provision, which this interpretation of the statute avoids. Of course, in deciding whether to credit Cheek's claim, the jury is free to consider any admissible evidence showing that he had knowledge of his legal duties. Pp. 609-612.

147

2. It was proper for the trial court to instruct the jury not to consider Cheek's claim that the tax laws are unconstitutional, since a defendant's views about the tax statutes' validity are irrelevant to the issue of willfulness and should not be heard by a jury. Unlike the claims in the *Murdock-Pomponio* line of cases, claims that Code provisions are unconstitutional do not arise from innocent mistakes caused by the Code's complexity. Rather, they reveal full knowledge of the provisions at issue and a studied conclusion that those provisions are invalid and unenforceable. Congress could not have contemplated that a taxpayer, without risking criminal prosecution, could ignore his duties under the Code and refuse to utilize the mechanisms Congress provided to present his invalidity claims to the courts and to abide by their decisions. Cheek was free to pay the tax, file for a refund, and, if denied, present his claims to the courts. Also, without paying the tax, he could have challenged claims of tax deficiencies in the Tax Court. Pp. 612-613.

882 F.2d 1263, (CA7 1989) vacated and remanded.

WHITE, J., delivered the opinion of the Court, in which REHNQUIST, C.J., and STEVENS, O'CONNOR, and KENNEDY, JJ., joined. SCALIA, J., filed an opinion concurring in the judgment. BLACKMUN, J., filed a dissenting opinion, in which MARSHALL, J., joined. SOUTER, J., took no part in the consideration or decision of the case.

William R. Coulson, Chicago, Ill., for petitioner.

Edwin S. Kneedler, Washington, D.C., for respondent.

Justice WHITE delivered the opinion of the Court.

Title 26, § 7201 of the United States Code provides that any person "who willfully attempts in any manner to evade or defeat any tax imposed by this title or the payment thereof" shall be guilty of a felony. Under 26 U.S.C. § 7203, "[a]ny person required under this title ... or by regulations made under authority thereof to make a return ... who willfully fails to ... make such return" shall be guilty of a misdemeanor. This case turns on the meaning of the word "willfully" as used in §§ 7201 and 7203.

I

Petitioner John L. Cheek has been a pilot for American Airlines since 1973. He filed federal income tax returns through 1979 but thereafter ceased to file returns.[1] He also claimed an increasing number of withholding allowances—eventually claiming 60 allowances by mid-1980—and for the years 1981 to 1984 indicated on his W-4 forms that he was exempt from federal income taxes. In 1983, petitioner unsuccessfully sought a refund of all tax withheld by his employer in 1982. Petitioner's income during this period at all times far exceeded the minimum necessary to trigger the statutory filing requirement.

As a result of his activities, petitioner was indicted for 10 violations of federal law. He was charged with six counts of willfully failing to file a federal income tax return for the years 1980, 1983, and 1986 through 1986, in violation of 26 U.S.C. § 7203. He was further charged with three counts of willfully attempting to evade his income taxes for the years 1980, 1981, and 1983 in violation of 26 U.S.C. § 7201. In those years, American Airlines withheld substantially less than the amount of tax petitioner owed because of the numerous allowances and exempt status he claimed on his W-4 forms.[2] The tax offenses with which petitioner was charged are specific intent crimes that require the defendant to have acted willfully.

At trial, the evidence established that between 1982 and 1986, petitioner was involved in at least four civil cases that challenged various aspects of the federal income tax system.[3] In all four of those cases, the plaintiffs were informed by the courts that many of their arguments, including that they were not taxpayers within the meaning of the tax laws, that wages are not income, that the Sixteenth Amendment does not authorize the imposition of an income tax on individuals, and that the Sixteenth Amendment is unenforceable, were frivolous or had been repeatedly rejected by the courts. During this time period, petitioner also attended at least two criminal trials of persons charged with tax offenses. In addition, there was evidence that in 1980 or 1981 an attorney had advised Cheek that the courts had rejected as frivolous the claim that wages are not income.[4]

Cheek represented himself at trial and testified in his defense. He admitted that he had not filed personal income tax returns during the years in question. He testified that as early as 1978, he had begun attending seminars sponsored by, and following the advice of, a group that believes, among other things, that the federal tax system is unconstitutional. Some of the speakers at these meetings were lawyers who purported to give professional opinions about the invalidity of the federal income tax laws. Cheek produced a letter from an attorney stating that the Sixteenth Amendment did not authorize a tax on wages and salaries but only on gain or profit. Petitioner's defense was that, based on the indoctrination he received from this group and from his own study, he sincerely believed that the tax laws were being unconstitutionally enforced and that his actions during the 1980-1986 period were lawful. He therefore argued that he had acted without the willfulness required for conviction of the various offenses with which he was charged.

In the course of its instructions, the trial court advised the jury that to prove "willfulness" the Government must prove the voluntary and intentional violation of a known legal duty, a burden that could not be proved by showing mistake, ignorance, or negligence. The court further advised the jury that an objectively reasonable good-faith misunderstanding of the law would negate willfulness but mere disagreement with the law would not. The court described Cheek's beliefs about the income tax system[5] and instructed the jury that if it found that Cheek "honestly and reasonably believed that he was not required to pay income taxes or to file tax returns," App. 81, a not guilty verdict should be returned.

After several hours of deliberation, the jury sent a note to the judge that stated in part:

" 'We have a basic disagreement between some of us as to if Mr. Cheek honestly & reasonably believed that he was not required to pay income taxes.

.   .   .   .   .

" 'Page 32 [the relevant jury instruction] discusses good faith misunderstanding & disagreement. Is there any additional clarification you can give us on this point?'" *Id.*, at 85.

The District Judge responded with a supplemental instruction containing the following statements:

"[A] person's opinion that the tax laws violate his constitutional rights does not constitute a good faith misunderstanding of the law. Furthermore, a person's disagreement with the government's tax collection systems and policies does not constitute a good faith misunderstanding of the law." *Id.*, at 86.

At the end of the first day of deliberation, the jury sent out another note saying that it still could not reach a verdict because " '[w]e are divided on the issue as to if Mr. Cheek honestly & reasonably believed that he was not required to pay income tax.'" *Id.*, at 87. When the jury resumed its deliberations, the District Judge gave the jury an additional instruction. This instruction stated in part that "[a]n honest but unreasonable belief is not a defense and does not negate willfulness," *id.*, at 88, and that "[a]dvice or research resulting in the conclusion that wages of a privately employed person are not income or that the tax laws are unconstitutional is not objectively reasonable and cannot serve as the basis for a good faith misunderstanding of the law defense." *Ibid.* The court also instructed the jury that "[p]ersistent refusal to acknowledge the law does not constitute a good faith misunderstanding of the law."

Ibid. Approximately two hours later, the jury returned a verdict finding petitioner guilty on all counts.[6]

Petitioner appealed his convictions, arguing that the District Court erred by instructing the jury that only an objectively reasonable misunderstanding of the law negates the statutory willfulness requirement. The United States Court of Appeals for the Seventh Circuit rejected that contention and affirmed the convictions. 882 F.2d 1263 (1989). In prior cases, the Seventh Circuit had made clear that good-faith misunderstanding of the law negates willfulness only if the defendant's beliefs are objectively reasonable; in the Seventh Circuit, even actual ignorance is not a defense unless the defendant's ignorance was itself objectively reasonable. See, *e.g., United States v. Buckner,* 830 F.2d 102 (1987). In its opinion in this case, the court noted that several specified beliefs, including the beliefs that the tax laws are unconstitutional and that wages are not income, would not be objectively reasonable.[7] Because the Seventh Circuit's interpretation of "willfully" as used in these statutes conflicts with the decisions of several other Courts of Appeals, see, *e.g., United States v. Whiteside,* 810 F.2d 1306, 1310-1311 (CA5 1987); *United States v. Phillips,* 775 F.2d 262, 263-264 (CA10 1985); *United States v. Aitken,* 755 F.2d 188, 191-193 (CA1 1985), we granted certiorari, 493 U.S. —, 110 S.Ct. 1108, 107 L.Ed.2d 1016 (1990).

II

[1.] The general rule that ignorance of the law or a mistake of law is no defense to criminal prosecution is deeply rooted in the American legal system. See, *e.g., United States v. Smith,* 5 Wheat. 153, 182, 5 L.Ed. 57 (1820) (Livingston, J., dissenting); *Barlow v. United States,* 7 Pet. 404, 411, 8 L.Ed. 728 (1833); *Reynolds v. United States,* 98 U.S. 145, 167, 25 L.Ed. 244 (1879); *Shevlin-Carpenter Co. v. Minnesota,* 218 U.S. 57, 68, 30 S.Ct. 663, 666, 54 L.Ed. 930 (1910); *Lambert v. California,* 355 U.S. 225, 228, 78 S.Ct. 240, 242, 2 L.Ed.2d 228 (1957); *Liparota v. United States,* 471 U.S. 419, 441, 105 S.Ct. 2084, 2096, 85 L.Ed.2d 434 (1985) (WHITE, J., dissenting); O. Holmes, The Common Law 47-48 (1881). Based on the notion that the law is definite and knowable, the common law presumed that every person knew the law. This common-law rule has been applied by the Court in numerous cases construing criminal statutes. See, e.g., *United States v. International Minerals & Chemical Corp.,* 402 U.S. 558, 91 S.Ct. 1697, 29 L.Ed.2d 178 (1971); *Hamling v. United States,* 418 U.S. 87, 119-124, 94 S.Ct. 2887, 2808-2911, 41 L.Ed.2d 590 (1974); *Boyce Motor Lines, Inc. v. United States,* 342 U.S. 337, 72 S.Ct. 329, 96 L.Ed. 367 (1952).

The proliferation of statutes and regulations has sometimes made it difficult for the average citizen to know and comprehend the extent of the duties and obligations imposed by the tax laws. Congress has accordingly softened the impact of the common-law presumption by making specific intent to violate the law an element of certain federal criminal tax offenses. Thus, the Court almost 60 years ago interpreted the statutory term "willfully" as used in the federal criminal tax statutes as carving out an exception to the traditional rule. This special treatment of criminal tax offenses is largely due to the complexity of the tax laws. In United States v. Murdock, 290 U.S. 389, 54 S.Ct 223, 78 L.Ed. 381 (1933), the Court recognized that:

"Congress did not intend that a person, by reason of a bona fide misunderstanding as to his liability for the tax, as to his duty to make a return, or as to the adequacy of the records he maintained, should become a criminal by his mere failure to measure up to the prescribed standard of conduct." *Id.*, at 396, 54 S.Ct., at 226.

The Court held that the defendant was entitled to an instruction with respect to whether he acted in good faith based on his actual belief. In *Murdock*, the Court interpreted the term "willfully" as used in the criminal tax statutes generally to mean "an act done with a bad purpose," *id.*, at 394, 54 S.Ct., at 225, or with "an evil motive." *Id.*, at 395, 54 S.Ct., at 225.

Subsequent decisions have refined this proposition. In *United States v. Bishop*, 412 U.S. 346, 93 S.Ct. 2008, 36 L.Ed.2d 941 (1973), we described the term "willfully" as connoting "a voluntary, intentional violation of a known legal duty," *id.*, at 360, 93 S.Ct., at 2017, and did so with specific reference to the "bad faith or evil intent" language employed in *Murdock*. Still later, *United States v. Pomponio*, 429 U.S. 10, 97 S.Ct. 22, 50 L.Ed.2d 12 (1976) (*per curiam*), addressed a situation in which several defendants had been charged with willfully filing false tax returns. The jury was given an instruction on willfulness similar to the standard set forth in *Bishop*. In addition, it was instructed that " '[g]ood motive alone is never a defense where the act done or omitted is a crime.'" *Id.*, at 11, 97 S.Ct., at 23. The defendants were convicted but the Court of Appeals reversed, concluding that the latter instruction was improper because the statute required a finding of bad purpose or evil motive. *Ibid.*

We reversed the Court of Appeals, stating that "the Court of Appeals incorrectly assumed that the reference to an 'evil motive' in *United States v. Bishop, supra*, and prior cases," *ibid.*, "requires proof of any motive other than an intentional violation of a known legal duty." Id., at 12, 97 S.Ct., at 23. As "the other Courts of Appeals that have considered the question have recognized, willfulness in this context simply means a voluntary, intentional violation of a known legal duty." *Ibid.* We concluded that after instructing the jury on willfulness, "[a]n additional instruction on good faith was unnecessary." *Id.*, at 13, 97 S.Ct., at 24. Taken together, *Bishop* and *Pomponio* conclusively establish that the standard for the statutory willfulness requirement is the "voluntary, intentional violation of a known legal duty."

III

Cheek accepts the *Pomponio* definition of willfulness, Brief for Petitioner 5, and n. 4, 13, 36; Reply Brief for Petitioner 4, 6-7, 11, 13, but asserts that the District Court's instructions and the Court of Appeals' opinion departed from that definition. In particular, he challenges the ruling that a good-faith misunderstanding of the law or a good-faith belief that one is not violating the law, if it is to negate willfulness, must be objectively reasonable. We agree that the Court of Appeals and the District Court erred in this respect.

A

[2-4] Willfulness, as construed by our prior decisions in criminal tax cases, requires the Government to prove that the law imposed a duty on the defendant, that the defendant knew of this duty, and that he voluntarily and intentionally violated that duty. We deal first with the case where the issue is whether the defendant knew of the duty purportedly imposed by the provision of the statute or regulation he is accused of violating, a case in which there is no claim that the provision at issue is invalid. In such a case, if the Government proves actual knowledge of the pertinent legal duty, the prosecution, without more, has satisfied the knowledge component of the willfulness requirement. But carrying this burden requires negating a defendant's claim of ignorance of the law or a claim that because of a misunderstanding of the law, he had a good-faith belief that he was not violating any of the provisions of the tax laws. This is so because one cannot be aware that the law imposes a duty upon him and yet be ignorant of it, misunderstand the law, or believe that the duty does not exist. In the end, the issue is whether, based on all the evidence, the Government has proved that the defendant was aware of the duty at issue, which cannot be true if the jury credits a good-faith misunderstanding and belief submission, whether or not the claimed belief or misunderstanding is objectively reasonable.

In this case, if Cheek asserted that he truly believed that the Internal Revenue Code did not purport to treat wages as income, and the jury believed him, the Government would not have carried its burden to prove willfulness, however unreasonable a court might deem such a belief. Of course, in deciding whether to credit Cheek's good-faith belief claim, the jury would be free to consider any admissible evidence from any source showing that Cheek was aware of his duty to file a return and to treat wages as income, including evidence showing his awareness of the relevant provisions of the Code or regulations, of court decisions rejecting his interpretation of the tax law, of authoritative rulings of the Internal Revenue Service, or of any contents of the personal income tax return forms and accompanying instructions that made it plain that wages should be returned as income.[8]

[5, 6] We thus disagree with the Court of Appeals' requirement that a claimed good-faith belief must be objectively reasonable if it is to be considered as possibly negating the Government's evidence purporting to show a defendant's awareness of the legal duty at issue. Knowledge and belief are characteristically questions for the factfinder, in this case the jury. Characterizing a particular belief as not objectively reasonable transforms the inquiry into a legal one and would prevent the jury from considering it. It would of course be proper to exclude evidence having no relevance or probative value with respect to willfulness; but it is not contrary to common sense, let alone impossible, for a defendant to be ignorant of his duty based on an irrational belief that he has no duty, and forbidding the jury to consider evidence that might negate willfulness would raise a serious question under the Sixth Amendment's jury trial provision. Cf. *Francis v. Franklin*, 471 U.S. 307, 105 S.Ct. 1965, 85 L.Ed.2d 344 (1985); *Sandstrom v. Montana*, 442 U.S. 510, 99 S.Ct. 2450, 61 L.Ed.2d 39 (1979); *Morissette v. United States*, 342 U.S. 246, 72 S.Ct. 240, 96 L.Ed. 288 (1952). It is common ground that this Court, where possible, interprets congressional enactments so as to avoid raising serious constitutional questions. See, *e.g., Edward J. DeBartolo Corp. v. Florida Gulf Coast Building and Construction Trades Council*, 485 U.S. 568, 575, 108 S.Ct. 1392, 1397, 99 L.Ed.2d 645 (1988); *Crowell v. Benson*, 285 U.S. 22, 62, and n. 30, 52 S.Ct. 285, 296, and n. 30, 76 L.Ed. 598 (1932); *Public Citizen v. United States Dept. of Justice*, 491 U.S. –, –, 109 S.Ct. 2558, 2572-2573, 105 L.Ed.2d 377 (1989).

[7] It was therefore error to instruct the jury to disregard evidence of Cheek's understanding that, within the meaning of the tax laws, he was not a person required to file a return or to pay income taxes and that wages are not taxable income, as incredible as such misunderstandings of and beliefs about the law might be. Of course, the more unreasonable the asserted beliefs or misunderstandings are, the more likely the jury will consider them to be nothing more than simple disagreement

with known legal duties imposed by the tax laws and will find that the Government has carried its burden of proving knowledge.

B

[8] Cheek asserted in the trial court that he should be acquitted because he believed in good faith that the income tax law is unconstitutional as applied to him and thus could not legally impose any duty upon him of which he should have been aware.[9] Such a submission is unsound, not because Cheek's constitutional arguments are not objectively reasonable or frivolous, which they surely are, but because the *Murdock-Pomponio* line of cases does not support such a position. Those cases construed the willfulness requirement in the criminal provisions of the Internal Revenue Code to require proof of knowledge of the law. This was because in "our complex tax system, uncertainty often arises even among taxpayers who earnestly wish to follow the law" and "'[i]t is not the purpose of the law to penalize frank difference of opinion or innocent errors made despite the exercise of reasonable care.'" *United States v. Bishop*, 412 U.S. 346, 360-361, 93 S.Ct. 2008, 2017-2018, 36 L.Ed.2d 941 (1973) (quoting *Spies v. United States*, 317 U.S. 492, 496, 63 S.Ct. 364, 367, 87 L.Ed. 418 (1943)).

Claims that some of the provisions of the tax code are unconstitutional are submissions of a different order.[10] They do not arise from innocent mistakes caused by the complexity of the Internal Revenue Code. Rather, they reveal full knowledge of the provisions at issue and a studied conclusion, however wrong, that those provisions are invalid and unenforceable. Thus in this case, Cheek paid his taxes for years, but after attending various seminars and based on his own study, he concluded that the income tax laws could not constitutionally require him to pay a tax.

We do not believe that Congress contemplated that such a taxpayer, without risking criminal prosecution, could ignore the duties imposed upon him by the Internal Revenue Code and refuse to utilize the mechanisms provided by Congress to present his claims of invalidity to the courts and to abide by their decisions. There is no doubt that Cheek, from year to year, was free to pay the tax that the law purported to require, file for a refund and, if denied, present his claims of invalidity, constitutional or otherwise, to the courts. See 26 U.S.C. § 7422. Also, without paying the tax, he could have challenged claims of tax deficiencies in the Tax Court, 26 U.S.C. § 6213, with the right to appeal to a higher court if unsuccessful. § 7482(a)(1). Cheek took neither course in some years, and when he did was unwilling to accept the outcome. As we see it, he is in no position to claim that his good-faith belief about the validity of the Internal Revenue Code negates willfulness or provides a defense to criminal prosecution under §§ 7201 and 7203. Of course, Cheek was free in this very case to present his claims of invalidity and have them adjudicated, but like defendants in criminal cases in other contexts, who "willfully" refuse to comply with the duties placed upon them by the law, he must take the risk of being wrong.

We thus hold that in a case like this, a defendant's views about the validity of the tax statutes are irrelevant to the issue of willfulness, need not be heard by the jury, and if they are, an instruction to disregard them would be proper. For this purpose, it makes no difference whether the claims of invalidity are frivolous or have substance. It was therefore not error in this case for the District Judge to instruct the jury not to consider Cheek's claims that the tax laws were unconstitutional. However, it was error for the court to instruct the jury that petitioner's asserted beliefs that wages are not income and that he was not a taxpayer within the meaning of the Internal Revenue Code should not be considered by the jury in determining whether Cheek had acted willfully.[11]

IV

For the reasons set forth in the opinion above, the judgment of the Court of Appeals is vacated, and the case is remanded for further proceedings consistent with this opinion.

It is so ordered.

Justice SOUTER took no part in the consideration or decision of this case.

Justice SCALIA, concurring in the judgment.

I concur in the judgment of Court because our cases have consistently held that the failure to pay a tax in the good-faith belief that it is not legally owing is not "willful." I do not join the Court's opinion because I do not agree with the test for willfulness that it directs the Court of Appeals to apply on remand.

As the Court acknowledges, our opinions from the 1930s to the 1970s have interpreted the word "willfully" in the criminal tax statutes as requiring the "bad purpose" or "evil motive" of "intentional[ly] violat[ing] a known legal duty." See, *e.g., United States v. Pomponio*, 429 U.S. 10, 12, 97 S.Ct. 22, 23, 50 L.Ed.2d 12 (1976); *United States v. Murdock*, 290 U.S. 389, 394-395, 54 S.Ct. 223, 225-226, 78 L.Ed. 381 (1933). It seems to me that today's opinion squarely reverses that long-established statutory construction when it says that a good-faith erroneous belief in the unconstitutionality of a tax law is no defense. It is quite impossible to say that a statute which one believes unconstitutional represents a "known legal duty." See *Marbury v. Madison*, 1 Cranch 137, 177-178, 2 L.Ed. 60 (1803).

Although the facts of the present case involve erroneous reliance upon the Constitution in ignoring the otherwise "known legal duty" imposed by the tax statutes, the Court's new interpretation applies also to erroneous reliance upon a tax statute in ignoring the otherwise "known legal duty" of a regulation, and to erroneous reliance upon a regulation in ignoring the otherwise "known legal duty" of a tax assessment. These situations as well meet the opinion's crucial test of "reveal[ing] full knowledge of the provisions at issue and a studied conclusion, however wrong, that those provisions are invalid and unenforceable," *ante*, at 613. There is, moreover, no rational basis for saying that a "willful" violation is established by full knowledge of a statutory requirement, but is not established by full knowledge of a requirement explicitly imposed by regulation or order. Thus, today's opinion works a revolution in past practice, subjecting to criminal penalties taxpayers who do not comply with Treasury Regulations that are in their view contrary to the Internal Revenue Code, Treasury Rulings that are in their view contrary to the regulations, and even IRS auditor pronouncements that are in their view contrary to Treasury Rulings. The law already provides considerable incentive for taxpayers to be careful in ignoring any official assertion of tax liability, since it contains civil penalties that apply even in the event of a good-faith mistake, see, *e.g.*, 26 U.S.C. §§ 6651, 6653. To impose in addition *criminal* penalties for misinterpretation of such a complex body of law is a startling innovation indeed.

I find it impossible to understand how one can derive from the lonesome word "willfully" the proposition that belief in the nonexistence of a textual prohibition excuses liability, but belief in the invalidity (*i.e.*, the legal nonexistence) of a textual prohibition does not. One may say, as the law does in many contexts, that "willfully" refers to consciousness of the act but not to consciousness that the act is unlawful. See, *e.g.*, *American Surety Co. of New York v. Sullivan*, 7 F.2d 605, 606 (CA2 1925) (L. Hand, J.); cf. *United States v. International Minerals and Chemical Co.*, 402 U.S. 558, 563-565, 91 S.Ct. 1697, 1700-1702, 29 L.Ed.2d 178 (1971). Or alternatively, one may say, as we have said until today with respect to the tax statutes, that "willfully" refers to consciousness of both the act *and* its illegality. But it seems to me impossible to say that the word refers to consciousness that some legal text exists, without consciousness that that legal text is binding, *i.e.*, with the good-faith belief that it is not a valid law. Perhaps such a test for criminal liability would make sense (though in a field as complicated as federal tax law, I doubt it), but some text other than the mere word "willfully" would have to be employed to describe it—and that text is not ours to write.

Because today's opinion abandons clear and long-standing precedent to impose criminal liability where taxpayers have had no reason to expect it, because the new contours of criminal liability have no basis in the statutory text, and because I strongly suspect that those new contours make no sense even as a policy matter, I concur only in the judgment of the Court.

Justice BLACKMUN, with whom Justice MARSHALL joins, dissenting.

It seems to me that we are concerned in this case not with "the complexity of the tax laws," *ante*, at 609, but with the income tax law in its most elementary and basic aspect: Is a wage earner a taxpayer and are wages income?

The Court acknowledges that the conclusively established standard for willfulness under the applicable statutes is the "voluntary, intentional violation of a known legal duty." Ante, at 610. See *United States v. Bishop*, 412 U.S. 346, 360, 93 S.Ct. 2008, 2017, 36 L.Ed.2d 941 (1963), and *United States v. Pomponio*, 429 U.S. 10, 12, 97 S.Ct. 22, 23, 50 L.Ed.2d 12 (1976). That being so, it is incomprehensible to me how, in this day, more than 70 years after the institution of our present federal income tax system with the passage of the Revenue Act of 1913, 38 Stat. 166, any taxpayer of competent mentality can assert as his defense to charges of statutory willfulness the proposition that the wage he receives for his labor is not income, irrespective of a cult that says otherwise and advises the gullible to resist income tax collections. One might note in passing that this particular taxpayer, after all, was a licensed pilot for one of our major commercial airlines; he presumably was a person of at least minimum intellectual competence.

The District Court's instruction that an objectively reasonable and good faith misunderstanding of the law negates willfulness lends further, rather than less, protection to this defendant, for it added an additional hurdle for the prosecution to overcome. Petitioner should be grateful for this further protection, rather than be opposed to it.

This Court's opinion today, I fear, will encourage taxpayers to cling to frivolous views of the law in the hope of convincing a jury of their sincerity. If that ensues, I suspect we have gone beyond the limits of common sense.

While I may not agree with every word the Court of Appeals has enunciated in its opinion, I would affirm its judgment in this case. I therefore dissent.

FOOTNOTES

*The syllabus constitutes no part of the opinion of the Court but has been prepared by the Reporter of Decisions for the convenience of the reader. See *United States v. Detroit Lumber Co.*, 200 U.S. 321, 337, 26 S.Ct. 282, 287, 50 L.Ed. 499.

1. Cheek did file what the Court of Appeals described as a frivolous return in 1982.

2. Because petitioner filed a refund claim for the entire amount withheld by his employer in 1982, petitioner was also charged under 18 U.S.C. § 287 with one count of presenting a claim to an agency of the United States knowing the claim to be false and fraudulent.

3. In March 1982, Cheek and another employee of the company sued American Airlines to challenge the withholding of federal income taxes. In April 1982, Cheek sued the IRS in the United States Tax court, asserting that he was not a taxpayer or a person for purposes of the Internal Revenue Code, that his wages were not income, and making several other related claims. Cheek and four others also filed an action against the United States and the CIR in Federal District Court, claiming that withholding taxes from their wages violated the Sixteenth Amendment. Finally, in 1985 Cheek filed claims with the IRS seeking to have refunded the taxes withheld from his wages in 1983 and 1984. When these claims were not allowed, he brought suit in the District Court claiming that the withholding was an unconstitutional taking of his property and that his wages were not income. In dismissing this action as frivolous, the District Court imposed costs and attorneys fees of $l,500 and a sanction under Rule 11 in the amount of $10,000. The Court of Appeals agreed that Cheek's claims were frivolous, reduced the District Court sanction to $5,000 and imposed an additional sanction of $l,500 for bringing a frivolous appeal.

4. The attorney also advised that despite the Fifth Amendment, the filing of a tax return was required and that a person could challenge the constitutionality of the system by suing for a refund after the taxes had been withheld, or by putting himself "at risk of criminal prosecution."

5. "The defendant has testified as to what he states are his interpretations of the United States Constitution, court opinions, common law and other materials he has reviewed ... He has also introduced materials which contain references to quotations from the United States Constitution, court opinions, statutes, and other sources.

"He testified he relied on his interpretations and on these materials in concluding that he was not a person required to file income tax returns for the year or years charged, was not required to pay income taxes and that he could claim exempt status on his W-4 forms, and that he could claim refunds of all moneys withheld." App. 75-76.

"Among other things, Mr. Cheek contends that his wages from a private employer, American Airlines, does not constitute income under the Internal Revenue Service laws." *Id.*, at 81.

6. A note signed by all 12 jurors also informed the judge that although the jury found petitioner guilty, several jurors wanted to express their personal opinions of the case and that notes from these individual jurors to the court were "a complaint against the narrow & hard expression under the constraints of the law." *Id.*, at 90. At least two notes from individual jurors expressed the opinion that petitioner sincerely believed in his cause even though his beliefs might have been unreasonable.

7. The opinion stated, 882 F.2d 1263, 1268-1269, n. 2 (CA7 1989), as follows:

"For the record, we note that the following beliefs, which are stock arguments of the tax protester movement, have not been, nor ever will be, considered 'objectively reasonable' in this circuit:

"(1) the belief that the sixteenth amendment to the constitution was improperly ratified and therefore never came into being;

"(2) the belief that the sixteenth amendment is unconstitutional generally;

"(3) the belief that the income tax violates the takings clause of the fifth amendment;

"(4) the belief that the tax laws are unconstitutional;

"(5) the belief that wages are not income and therefore are not subject to federal income tax laws;

"(6) the belief that filing a tax return violates the privilege against self-incrimination; and

"(7) the belief that Federal Reserve Notes do not constitute cash or income.

"*Miller v. United States*, 868 F.2d 236, 239-41 (7th Cir.1989); *Buckner*, 830 F.2d at 102; *United States v. Dube*, 820 F.2d 886, 891 (7th Cir.1987); *Coleman v. Comm'r*, 791 F.2d 68, 70-71 (7th Cir.1986); *Moore*, 627 F.2d at 833. We have no doubt that this list will increase with time."

8. Cheek recognizes that a "defendant who knows what the law is and who disagrees with it . . . does not have a bona fide misunderstanding defense" but asserts that "a defendant who has a bona fide misunderstanding of [the law] does not 'know' his legal duty and lacks willfulness." Brief for Petitioner 29, and n. 13. The Reply Brief for Petitioner, at 13, states: "We are in no way suggesting that Cheek or anyone else is immune from criminal prosecution if he knows what the law is, but believes it should be otherwise, and therefore violates it." See also Tr. of Oral Arg. 9, 11, 12, 15, 17.

9. In his opening and reply briefs and at oral argument, Cheek asserts that this case does not present the issue of whether a claim of unconstitutionality would serve to negate willfulness and that we need not address the issue. Brief for Petitioner 13; Reply Brief for Petitioner 5, 11, 12; Tr. of Oral Arg. 6, 13. Cheek testified at trial, however, that "[i]t is my belief that the law

is being enforced unconstitutionally." App. 60. He also produced a letter from counsel advising him that " 'Finally you make a valid contention ... that Congress' power to tax comes from Article I, Section 8, Clause 1 of the U.S. Constitution, and not from the Sixteenth Amendment and that the [latter], construed with Article I, Section 2, Clause 3, never authorized a tax on wages and salaries, but only on gain and profit." *Id.*, at 57. We note also that the jury asked for "the portion [of the transcript] wherein Mr. Cheek stated he was attempting to test the constitutionality of the income tax laws," Tr. 1704, and that the trial judge later instructed the jury that an opinion that the tax laws violate a person's constitutional rights does not constitute a good faith misunderstanding of the law. We also note that at oral argument Cheek's counsel observed that "personal belief that a known statute is unconstitutional smacks of knowledge with existing law, but disagreement with it." Tr. of Oral Arg. 5. He also opined that:

"If the person believes as a personal belief that known—law known to them *[sic]* is unconstitutional, I submit that that would not be a defense, because what the person is really saying is I know what the law is, for constitutional reasons I have made my own determination that it is invalid. I am not suggesting that that is a defense.

"However, if the person was told by a lawyer or by an accountant erroneously that the statute is unconstitutional, and it's my professional advice to you that you don't have to follow it, then you have got a little different situation. This is not that case." *Id.*, at 6.

Given this posture of the case, we perceive no reason not to address the significance of Cheek's constitutional claims to the issue of willfulness.

10. In *United States v. Murdock*, 290 U.S. 389, 54 S.Ct. 223, 78 L.Ed. 381 (1933), discussed *supra*, at 609-610, the defendant Murdock was summoned to appear before a revenue agent for examination. Questions were put to him, which he refused to answer for fear of self-incrimination under state law. He was indicted for refusing to give testimony and supply information contrary to the pertinent provisions of the Internal Revenue Code. This Court affirmed the reversal of Murdock's conviction, holding that the trial court erred in refusing to give an instruction directing the jury to consider Murdock's asserted claim of a good-faith, actual belief that because of the Fifth Amendment he was privileged not to answer the questions put to him. It is thus the case that Murdock's asserted belief was grounded in the Constitution, but it was a claim of privilege not to answer, not a claim that any provision of the tax laws were unconstitutional, and not a claim for which the tax laws provided procedures to entertain and resolve. Cheek's position at trial, in contrast, was that the tax laws were unconstitutional as applied to him.

11. Cheek argues that applying to him the Court of Appeals' standard of objective reasonableness violates his rights under the First, Fifth, and Sixth Amendments of the Constitution. Since we have invalidated the challenged standard on statutory grounds, we need not address these submissions.

Cite: 680 Fed Rptr 2d 1240 (1982)

John L. LEWIS, Plaintiff/Appellant,
v.
UNITED STATES of America,
Defendant/Appellee.
No. 80-5905.
United States Court of Appeals,
Ninth Circuit.
Submitted March 2, 1982.
Decided April 19, 1982.
As Amended June 24, 1982.

Plaintiff, who was injured by vehicle owned and operated by a federal reserve bank, brought action alleging jurisdiction under the Federal Tort Claims Act. The United States District Court for the Central District of California, David W. Williams, J., dismissed holding that federal reserve bank was not a federal agency within meaning of Act and that the court therefore lacked subject-matter jurisdiction. Appeal was taken. The Court of Appeals, Poole, Circuit Judge, held that federal reserve banks are not federal instrumentalities for purposes of the Act, but are independent, privately owned and locally controlled corporations.

Affirmed.

1. United States #78(4)

There are no sharp criteria for determining whether an entity is a federal agency within meaning of the Federal Tort Claims Act, but critical factor is existence of federal government control over "detailed physical performance" and "day to day operation" of an entity. 28 U.S.C.A. §§ 1346(b), 2671 et seq.

2. United States #78(4)

Federal reserve banks are not federal instrumentalities for purposes of a Federal Tort Claims Act, but are independent, privately owned and locally controlled corporations in light of fact that direct supervision and control of each bank is exercised by board of directors, federal reserve banks, though heavily regulated, are locally controlled by their

(#) = West Key number system. For other cases see same topic & KEY-NUMBER in all Key-Numbered Digests & Indexes.

member banks, banks are listed neither as "wholly owned" government corporations nor as "mixed ownership" corporations; federal reserve banks receive no appropriated funds from Congress and the banks are empowered to sue and be sued in their own names. 28 U.S.C.A. §§ 1346(b), 2671 et seq.; Federal Reserve Act, §§ 4, 10(a, b), 13, 13a, 13b, 14, 14 (a-g), 16, 12 U.S.C.A. §§ 301, 341-360; 12 U.S.C.A. § 361; Government Corporation Control Act, §§ 101, 201, 31 U.S.C.A. §§ 846, 856.

3. United States #78(4)
Under the Federal Tort Claims Act, federal liability is narrowly based on traditional agency principles and does not necessarily lie when a tortfeasor simply works for an entity, like the Reserve Bank, which performs important activities for the government. 28 U.S.C.A. §§ 1346(b), 2671 et seq.

4. Taxation #6
The Reserve Banks are deemed to be federal instrumentalities for purposes of immunity from state taxation.

5. States #4.15
Taxation #6
Tests for determining whether an entity is federal instrumentality for purposes of protection from state or local action or taxation, is very broad: whether entity performs important governmental function.

Lafayette L. Blair, Compton, Cal., for plaintiff/appellant.

James R. Sullivan, Asst. U. S. Atty., Los Angeles, Cal., argued, for defendant/appellee; Andrea Sheridan Ordin, U. S. Atty., Los Angeles, Cal., on brief.

Appeal from the United States District Court for the Central District of California.

Before POOLE and BOOCHEVER, Circuit Judges, and SOLOMON, District Judge. •

POOLE, Circuit Judge:
On July 27, 1979, appellant John Lewis was injured by a vehicle owned and operated by the Los Angeles branch of the Federal Reserve Bank of San Francisco. Lewis brought this action in district court

alleging jurisdiction under the Federal Tort Claims Act (the Act), 28 U.S.C. § 1346(b). The United States moved to dismiss for lack of subject matter jurisdiction. The district court dismissed, holding that the Federal Reserve Bank is not a federal agency within the meaning of the Act and that the court therefore lacked subject mater jurisdiction. We affirm.

In enacting the Federal Tort Claims Act, Congress provided a limited waiver of the sovereign immunity of the United States for certain torts of federal employees. *United States v. Orleans*, 425 U.S. 807, 813, 96 S.Ct. 1971, 1975, 48 L.Ed.2d 390 (1976). Specifically, the Act creates liability for injuries "caused by the negligent or wrongful act or omission" of an employee of any federal agency acting within the scope of his office or employment. 28 U.S.C. §§ 1346(b), 2671. "Federal agency" is defined as:

> the executive departments, the military departments, independent establishments of the United States, and corporations acting primarily as instrumentalities of the United States, but does not include any contractors with the United States.

28 U.S.C. § 2671. The liability of the United States for the negligence of a Federal Reserve Bank employee depends, therefore, on whether the Bank is a federal agency under § 2671.

[1, 2] There are no sharp criteria for determining whether an entity is a federal agency within the meaning of the Act, but the critical factor is the existence of federal government control over the "detailed physical performance" and "day to day operation" of that entity. *United States v. Orleans*, 425 U.S. 807, 814, 96 S.Ct. 1971, 1975, 48 L.Ed.2d 390 (1976), *Logue v. United States*, 412 U.S. 521, 528, 93 S.Ct 2215, 2219, 37 L.Ed.2d 121 (1973). Other factors courts have considered include whether the entity is an independent corporation, *Pearl v. United States*, 230 F.2d 243 (10th Cir. 1956), *Freeling v. Federal Deposit Insurance Corporation*, 221 F.Supp. 955 (W.D. Okla.1962), *aff'd per curiam*, 326 F.2d 971 (10th Cir. 1963), whether the government is involved in the entity's finances. *Goddard v. District of Columbia Redevelopment Land Agency*, 287 F.2d 343, 345 (D.C.Cir. 1961), *cert. denied*, 366 U.S. 910, 81 S.Ct. 1085, 6 L.Ed.2d 235 (1961), *Freeling v. Federal Deposit Insurance Corporation*, 221 F.Supp. 955, and whether the mission of the entity furthers the policy of the United States, *Goddard v. District of Columbia Redevelopment Land Agency*, 287 F.2d at 345. Examining the organization and function of the Federal Reserve Banks, and applying the relevant factors, we conclude that the Reserve Banks are not federal instrumentalities for purposes of the FTCA, but are independent, privately owned and locally controlled corporations.

Each Federal Reserve Bank is a separate corporation owned by commercial banks in its region. The stockholding commercial banks elect two thirds of each Bank's nine member board of directors. The remaining three directors are appointed by the Federal Reserve Board. The Federal Reserve Board regulates the Reserve Banks, but direct supervision and control of each Bank is exercised by its board of directors. 12 U.S.C. § 301. The directors enact by-laws regulating the manner of conducting general Bank business, 12 U.S.C. § 341, and appoint officers to implement and supervise daily Bank activities. These activities include collecting and clearing checks, making advances to private and commercial entities, holding reserves for member banks, discounting the notes of member banks, and buying and selling securities on the open market. *See* 12 U.S.C. §§ 341-361.

Each Bank is statutorily empowered to conduct these activities without day to day direction from the federal government. Thus, for example, the interest rates on advances to member banks, individuals, partnerships, and corporations are set by each Reserve Bank and their decisions regarding the purchase and sale of securities are likewise independently made.

It is evident from the legislative history of the Federal Reserve Act that Congress did not intend to give the federal government direction over the daily operation of the Reserve Banks:

It is proposed that the Government shall retain sufficient power over the reserve banks to enable it to exercise a direct authority when necessary to do so, but that it shall in no way attempt to carry on through its own mechanism the routine operations and banking which require detailed knowledge of local and individual credit and which determine the funds of the community in any given instance. In other words, the reserve-bank plan retains to the Government power over the exercise of the broader banking functions, while it leaves to individuals and privately owned institutions the actual direction of routine.

H.R. Report No. 69, 63 Cong. 1st Sess. 18-19 (1913).

The fact that the Federal Reserve Board regulates the Reserve Banks does not make them federal agencies under the Act. In *United States v. Orleans*, 425 U.S. 807, 96 S.Ct. 1971, 48 L.Ed.2d 390 (1976), the Supreme Court held that a community action agency was not a federal agency or instrumentality for purposes of the Act, even though the agency was organized under federal regulations and heavily funded by the federal government. Because the agency's day to day operation was not supervised by the federal government, but by local officials, the Court refused to extend federal tort liability for the negligence of the agency's employees. Similarly, the Federal Reserve Banks, though heavily regulated, are locally controlled by their member banks. Unlike typical federal agencies, each bank is empowered to hire and fire employees at will. Bank employees do not participate in the Civil Service Retirement System. They are covered by worker's compensation insurance, purchased by the Bank, rather than the Federal Employees Compensation Act. Employees traveling on Bank business are not subject to federal travel regulations and do not receive government employee discounts on lodging and services.

The Banks are listed neither as "wholly owned" government corporations under 31 U.S.C. § 846 nor as "mixed ownership" corporations under 31 U.S.C. § 856, a factor considered in *Pearl v. United States*, 230 F.2d 243 (10th Cir. 1956), which held that the Civil Air Patrol is not a federal agency under the Act. Closely resembling the status of the Federal Reserve Bank, the Civil Air Patrol is a non-profit, federally chartered corporation organized to serve the public welfare. But because Congress' control over the Civil Air Patrol is limited and the corporation is not designated as a wholly owned or mixed ownership government corporation under 31 U.S.C. §§ 846 and 856, the court concluded that the corporation is a non-governmental, independent entity, not covered under the Act.

Additionally, Reserve Banks, as privately owned entities, receive no appropriated funds from Congress. *Cf. Goddard v. District of Columbia Redevelopment Land Agency*, 287 F.2d. 343, 345 (D.C.Cir.1961), *cert. denied*, 366 U.S. 910, 81 S.Ct. 1085, 6 L.Ed.2d 235 (1961) (court held land redevelopment agency was federal agency for purposes of the Act in large part because agency received direct appropriated funds from Congress.)

Finally, the Banks are empowered to sue and be sued in their own name. 12 U.S.C. § 341. They carry their own liability insurance and typically process and handle their own claims. In the past, the Banks have defended against tort claims directly, through private counsel, not government attorneys, *e.g., Banco De Espana v. Federal Reserve Bank of New York*, 114 F.2d 438 (2d Cir. 1940); *Huntington Towers v. Franklin National Bank*, 559 F.2d 863 (2d Cir. 1977); *Bollow v. Federal Reserve Bank of San Francisco*, 650 F.2d 1093 (9th Cir. 1981), and they have never been required to settle tort claims under the administrative procedure of 28 U.S.C. § 2672. The waiver of sovereign immunity contained in the Act would therefore appear to be inapposite to the Banks who have not historically claimed or received general immunity from judicial process.

[3] The Reserve Banks have properly been held to be federal instrumentalities for some purposes. In *United States v. Hollingshead,* 672 F2.d 751 (9th Cir. 1982), this court held that a Federal Reserve Bank employee who was responsible for recommending expenditure of federal funds was a "public official" under the Federal Bribery Statute. That statute broadly defines public official to include any person acting "for or on behalf of the Government." S. Rep. No. 2213, 87th Cong., 2nd Sess. (1962), *reprinted in* [1962] U.S. Code Cong. & Ad. News 3852, 3856. *See* 18 U.S.C. § 201(a). The test for determining status as a public official turns on whether there is "substantial federal involvement" in the defendant's activities. *United States v. Hollingshead,* 672 F.2d at 754. In contrast, under the FTCA, federal liability is narrowly based on traditional agency principles and does not necessarily lie when the tortfeasor simply works for an entity, like the Reserve Banks, which perform important activities for the government.

[4, 5] The Reserve Banks are deemed to be federal instrumentalities for purposes of immunity from state taxation. *Federal Reserve Bank of Boston v. Commissioner of Corporations & Taxation,* 499 F.2d 60 (1st Cir. 1974), *after remand,* 520 F.2d 221 (1st Cir. 1975); *Federal Reserve Bank of Minneapolis v. Register of Deeds,* 288 Mich. 120, 284 N.W. 667 (1939). The test for determining whether an entity is a federal instrumentality for purposes of protection from state or local action or taxation, however, is very broad: whether the entity performs an important governmental function. *Federal Land Bank v. Bismarck Lumber Co.,* 314 U.S. 95, 102, 62 S.Ct. 1, 5, 86 L.Ed. 65 (1941); *Rust v. Johnson,* 597 F.2d 174, 178 (9th Cir. 1979), *cert. denied,* 444 U.S. 964, 100 S.Ct. 450, 62 L.Ed.2d 376 (1979). The Reserve Banks, which further the nation's fiscal policy, clearly perform an important governmental function.

Performance of an important governmental function, however, is but a single factor and not determinative in tort claims actions. *Federal Reserve Bank of St. Louis v. Metrocentre Improvement District,* 657 F.2d 183, 185 n.2 (8th Cir. 1981), *Cf. Pearl v. United States,* 230 F.2d 243 (10th Cir. 1956). State taxation has traditionally been viewed as a greater obstacle to an entity's ability to perform federal functions than exposure to judicial process; therefore tax immunity is liberally applied. *Federal Land Bank v. Priddy,* 294 U.S. 229, 235, 55 S.Ct. 705, 708, 79 L.Ed. 1408 (1955). Federal tort liability, however, is based on traditional agency principles and thus depends upon the principal's ability to control the actions of his agent, and not simply upon whether the entity performs an important governmental function. *See United States v.*

Orleans, 425 U.S. 807, 815, 96 S.Ct. 1971, 1976, 48 L.Ed.2d 390 (1976), *United States v. Logue*, 412 U.S. 521, 527-28, 93 S.Ct. 2215, 2219, 37 L.Ed.2d 121 (1973).

Brinks Inc. v. Board of Governors of the Federal Reserve System, 466 F.Supp. 116 (D.D.C.1979), held that a Federal Reserve Bank is a federal instrumentality for purposes of the Service Contract Act, 41 U.S.C. § 351. Citing *Federal Reserve Bank of Boston* and *Federal Reserve Bank of Minneapolis*, the court applied the "important governmental function" test and concluded that the term "Federal Government" in the Service Contract Act must be "liberally construed to effectuate the Act's humanitarian purposes of providing minimum wage and fringe benefit protection to individuals performing contracts with the federal government." *Id.* 288 Mich. at 120, 284 N.W.2d 667.

Such a liberal construction of the term "federal agency" for purposes of the Act is unwarranted. Unlike in *Brinks*, plaintiffs are not without a forum in which to seek a remedy, for they may bring an appropriate state tort claim directly against the Bank; and if successful, their prospects of recovery are bright since the institutions are both highly solvent and amply insured.

For these reasons we hold that the Reserve Banks are not federal agencies for purposes of the Federal Tort Claims Act and we affirm the judgment of the district court.

AFFIRMED.

Footnotes
•The Honorable Gus J. Solomon, Senior District Judge for the District of Oregon, sitting by designation.

Cite: 281 Fed Rptr 236 (1922)

LONG v. RASMUSSEN, Collector of Internal Revenue, et al.
(District Court, D. Montana. May 29, 1922.)

No. 97.

1. Internal revenue #28—Prima facie proof property was owned by
claimant puts burden on collector to prove it belonged to taxpayer.

In a suit to enjoin the collector of internal revenue from selling
property claimed by plaintiff under distraint to enforce taxes levied
against another, evidence on behalf of plaintiff that the property
comprised the furnishings of a hotel conducted by her, which was
in her possession when distrained, was proof of her ownership and
right of possession, which imposed on the defendant the burden to
justify the seizure by a preponderance of evidence showing that
the property belonged to the taxpayer.

2. Internal revenue #28—Evidence held to show property distrained did
not belong to taxpayer.

In a suit to restrain the sale of property claimed by plaintiff for
taxes and penalties assessed against another, where plaintiff had
made a prima facie case of ownership and right to possession,
evidence on behalf of the collector *held* insufficient to show that
the property distrained was that of the taxpayer.

3. Evidence #99—Lists of property returned for taxes are generally
inadmissible against other parties.

On the issue of ownership of personal property between a
claimant of the property and the collector of internal revenue, who
had distrained it as the property of a taxpayer, tax lists returned by
the taxpayer to the assessor of local taxes, including the property in
controversy, are generally incompetent as res inter allos acta.

4. Internal revenue #28—Threatened seizure of property, which would
interrupt going business, may be enjoined.

An injunction may be issued to restrain the collector of internal
revenue from seizing the property of plaintiff for the taxes owing
by another, where such seizures threaten disruption of plaintiff's
going business, resulting in the indiction of uncertain damages and
irreparable injury.

(#) = West Key number system. For other cases see same topic & KEY-
NUMBER in all Key-Numbered Digests & Indexes.

5. United States #125—Suit to enjoin distraint by collector is not suit against United States.

A suit against the collector of internal revenue to enjoin sale by him under distraint proceedings of property claimed by plaintiff for taxes assessed against another is not a suit against the United States, but is against an individual who, as an officer in discharge of a discretionless ministerial duty, is committing trespass on plaintiff's property without authority.

6. Internal revenue #28—Statute against restraining collection of taxes applies only to suits by taxpayer.

Rev. St. § 3224 (Comp. St. § 5947), prohibiting suit to restrain the collection of any tax, applies to suits by taxpayers only, who are given a remedy by section 3226 (Comp. St. § 5949), and does not prohibit an injunction against sale under distraint of the property belonging to plaintiff to satisfy taxes assessed against another.

7. Internal revenue #28—Statute against restraining collection of taxes applies only to those within scope of revenue laws.

Rev. St. § 3224 (Comp. St. § 5947), prohibiting suits to enjoin the collection of taxes, applies only to persons and things within the scope of the revenue laws, and not to those without such scope.

8. Internal revenue #28—Prevention of replevin of property distrained does not prevent injunction against sale.

Rev. St. § 934 (Comp. St. § 1560), making irrepleviable property taken by an officer under authority of any revenue law, and making such property in custody of law subject only to decrees of the courts of the United States, probably prevents replevin of property seized by the collector of internal revenue to satisfy taxes levied against one not the owner; but the owner of the property is left free to bring any other proper action to determine the owner-ship and possession of the property.

In Equity. Suit by Edna Long against C. A. Rasmussen, Collector of Internal Revenue for the District of Montana, and another. Decree rendered for plaintiff.

George F. Shelton, J. Bruce Kremer, L. P. Sanders, and Alf C. Kremer, all of Butte, Mont., for plaintiff.

John L Slattery, U. S. Dist. Atty., of Helena, Mont., for defendants.

BOURQUIN, District Judge. Plaintiff alleges she owns and is entitled to possession of certain property distrained by defendant collector of internal revenue, to make certain "distilled spirits taxes and penalties" assessed against one Wise, and she seeks to enjoin threatened sale and to recover possession.

[1] The evidence in her behalf is that the property is the furnishings of a resort or hotel conducted by her, excepting an automatic organ is owned by her, and was in her possession when distrained by defendant. This is proof of plaintiff's ownership and right of possession, and imposes upon defendant the burden to justify the seizure by a preponderance of the evidence that Wise owns the property.

[2] To that end he presents ambiguous circumstances only, viz. that Wise or his wife has some interest in the hotel building; that during plaintiff's tenancy of the building Wise once gave his address as at that hotel, had installed the automatic organ, and made payments upon it, and in 1917-1921 presented to the assessor of local taxes lists of property for taxation to Wise, including the hotel building and furnishings, which taxes were paid by him. These lists were admitted, subject to the anomalous objection that they be "taken only for what they are worth."

[3, 4] Being res inter alios acta, the better rule is that generally they are not competent evidence in actions involving title and ownership of property, and to which the list maker is not a party. In any event, the burden has not been sustained by defendant, and the finding is that at time of seizure and now plaintiff was and is owner and entitled to possession of the property. To dispose briefly of various suggestions, rather than contentions, the seizure threatening disruption of plaintiff's going business, infliction of uncertain damages, and irreparable injury, equity has jurisdiction, even as in like circumstances of wrongful attachment or execution, for that law affords no adequate remedy. See Watson v. Sutherland, 5 Wall. 79, 18 L. Ed. 580.

[5] The suit is not against the United States, but is against an individual who, as an officer of the United States in discharge of a discretionless ministerial duty, upon plaintiff's property is committing without authority, contrary to his duty, and in violation of the due process of the Constitution and the revenue laws of the United States, positive acts of trespass for which he is personally liable. See Philadelphia Co. v. Stimson, 223 U. S. 620, 32 Sup. Ct. 340, 56 L. Ed. 570; Belknap v. Schild, 161 U. S. 18, 16 Sup. Ct. 443, 40 L. Ed. 599; U.S. v. Lee, 106 U. S. 219, 1 Sup. Ct. 240, 27 L. Ed. 171; Magruder v. Association, 219 Fed. 78, 135 C. C. A. 524. Congress has no power to grant, and has not assumed to grant, authority to the defendant collector to distrain the property of one person to make the taxes of another. Perhaps it could, were the property in possession of the taxpayer, which is not this case. See Sears v. Cottrell, 5 Mich. 253.

[6] Section 3224, R. S. (Comp. St. § 5947), that "no suit for the purpose of restraining the assessment or collection of any tax shall be maintained in any court," applies to taxpayers only, and who, thus deprived of one remedy, are given another by section 3226, R. S. (Comp. St. § 5949), viz. an action to recover after taxes paid and repayment denied by the Commissioner. Nor are they limited to this statutory remedy, but, after taxes paid, they may have trespass or other action against the collector. See Erskine v. Hohnbach, 14 Wall. 616, 20 L. Ed. 745; De Lima v. Bidwell, 182 U. S. 179, 21 Sup. Ct. 743, 45 L. Ed. 1041; Pacific Co. v. U. S., 187 U. S. 453, 23 Sup. Ct. 154, 47 L. Ed. 253.

The revenue laws are a code or system in regulation of tax assessment and collection. They relate to taxpayers, and not to nontaxpayers. The latter are without their scope. No procedure is prescribed for nontaxpayers, and no attempt is made to annul any of their rights and remedies in due course of law. With them Congress does not assume to deal, and they are neither of the subject nor of the object of the revenue laws. The instant suit is not to restrain assessment or collection of taxes of Wise, but is to enjoin trespass upon property of plaintiff, and against whom no assessment has been made, and of whom no collection is sought. Note, too, the taxes are not assessed against the property. This presents a widely different case than that wherein the person assessed, or whose property is assessed, seeks to restrain assessment or collection on the theory that he or it is exempt from taxation, or that for any reason the tax is illegal.

[7] The distinction between persons and things within the scope of the revenue laws and those without them is vital. See De Lima v. Bidwell, 182 U. S. 176, 179, 21 Sup. Ct. 743, 45 L. Ed. 1041. To the former only does section 3224 apply (see cases cited in Violette v. Walsh [D. C.] 272 Fed. 1016), and the well-understood exigencies of government and its revenues and their collection do not serve to extend it to the latter. It is a shield for official action, not a sword for private aggression. There is dictum to the contrary in Sheridan v. Allen, 153 Fed. 569, 82 C. C. A. 522, but it is neither supported by the case it cites nor by any other brought to attention.

[8] Markle v. Kirkendall (D. C.) 267 Fed. 500, tends to the conclusion herein. It is not improbable that section 934, R. S. (Comp. St. § 1560), wherein it provides that property taken by an officer "under authority of any revenue law" is "irrepleviable," is in "custody of law," and "subject only to the orders and decrees of the courts of the United States having jurisdiction thereof," contemplates the instant case. The collector assumed in good faith to distrain property he believes to be the taxpayer's. If he peaceably secures possession of it (for, if not the

taxpayer's, the owner may lawfully forcibly prevent), he is not bound to deliver it to any chance claimant, nor is he subject to be deprived of it by replevin before trial.

The nontaxpayer owner, however, is free to bring any other proper action, the court to determine title, ownership, and possession, the collector having no power to do so, and the property "subject only to the orders and decrees of the court," to be by the court disposed of as justice requires. See In re Fassett, 142 U. S. 486, 12 Sup. Ct. 295, 35 L. Ed. 1087; De Lima v. Bidwell, 182 U. S. 180, 21 Sup. Ct. 743, 45 L. Ed. 1041. And this is the course in respect to any property in custodia legis, aside from statute.

This trial demonstrating that plaintiff owns and is entitled to possession of the property, and that the defendant wrongfully seized it to make taxes owed by Wise, justice requires that the sale be enjoined and the possession restored to her.

Decree accordingly, and with costs.

ABOUT THE AUTHOR

Barrie Konicov, best known as the author and voice of Potentials Unlimited tapes, wrote and recorded over 200 self-hypnosis/subliminal persuasion tapes beginning in the late 1970s. Acknowledged by his peers as one of the premier hynotherapists in the world, Barrie's work has set the standard for hypnosis and subliminal tapes worldwide.

Barrie and his wife, Susie, started Connecting Link magazine in 1988. Then, in 1990, they stopped filing and paying federal, state and Social Security taxes. That same year (after educating themselves and researching the income tax system), they filed a series of documents with the government that resulted in the I.R.S. notifying Susie that they agreed with her information and that she did not have to file or pay federal income tax. A copy of this letter is found on page18. As an outgrowth of this experience, Barrie began marketing detaxing programs and founded De-Taxing America. In May of 1994, he accepted the Libertarian nomination for United States Congressman for the Third District of Michigan. While he lost the seat to the incumbent, his message about the fraud in our current tax and money systems was and continues to be brought to many.

Barrie can be reached at De-Taxing America, 9392 Whitneyville Rd. S.E., Alto, Mich. 49302. Tel: (616) 891-2217 FAX: (616) 891-1450.